Bravo, Teacher!

Building Relationships *with Actions* that Value Others

Sandra Harris

Routledge
Taylor & Francis Group

LONDON AND NEW YORK

First published 2005 by Eye on Education

Published 2013 by Routledge
2 Park Square, Milton Park, Abingdon, Oxon OX14 4RN
711 Third Avenue, New York, NY, 10017, USA

Routledge is an imprint of the Taylor & Francis Group, an informa business

Library of Congress Cataloging-in-Publication Data
 Harris, Sandra, 1946-
 Bravo, teacher! : building relationships with actions that value others / Sandra Harris.
  p. cm.
 Includes bibliographical references.
 ISBN 1-59667-012-6
 1. Teachers – Professional relationships. 2. Teacher – student relationships. 3. Educational leadersh
 I. Ti tle.
 LB1775.H33 2006
                                                                    371.1—dc2

ISBN 13: 978-1-596-67012-9 (pbk)

Editorial and production services provided by Richard H. Adin Freelance Editorial Services

Also Available from EYE ON EDUCATION

BRAVO Principal!
Building Relationships with
Actions That Value Others
Sandra Harris

What Great Teachers Do Differently:
14 Things That Matter Most
Todd Whitaker

Classroom Motivation from A to Z:
How To Engage Your Students in Learning
Barbara R. Blackburn

Great Quotes for Great Educators
Todd Whitaker and Dale Lumpa

What Great Principals Do Differently:
15 Things That Matter Most
Todd Whitaker

101 "Answers" for New Teachers and Their Mentors:
Effective Teaching Tips for Daily Classroom Use
Annette L. Breaux

Talk It Out!
The Educator's Guide
to Successful Difficult Conversations
Barbara E. Sanderson

Differentiated Instruction:
A Guide for Elementary School Teachers
Amy Benjamin

Handbook on Differentiated Instruction
for Middle and High Schools
Sheryn Spencer Northey

What Successful Principals Do!
169 Tips for Principals
Franzy Fleck

Motivating & Inspiring Teachers:
The Educational Leader's Guide for Building Staff Morale
Todd Whitaker, Beth Whitaker, and Dale Lumpa

Dealing with Difficult Parents
(And with Parents in Difficult Situations)
Todd Whitaker and Douglas Fiore

Dealing with Difficult Teachers, Second Edition
Todd Whitaker

20 Strategies for Collaborative School Leaders
Jane Clark Lindle

The Principal as Instructional Leader:
A Handbook for Supervisors
Sally J. Zepeda

Instructional Leadership for School Improvement
Sally J. Zepeda

Six Types of Teachers: Recruiting, Retaining,
and Mentoring the Best
Douglas J. Fiore and Todd Whitaker

Supervision Across the Content Areas
Sally J. Zepeda and R. Stewart Mayers

The Administrator's Guide to School
Community Relations, 2nd Edition
George E. Pawlas

Stepping Outside Your Comfort Zone:
Lessons for School Leaders
Nelson Beaudoin

Data Analysis for Continuous School Improvement
Victoria L. Bernhardt

Handbook on Teacher Evaluation:
Assessing and Improving Performance
James Stronge and Pamela Tucker

Table of Contents

Introduction

Make the Most of a Moment

We had gotten up early and driven from Waterford, Ireland, to Rosslaire to ferry back to England. It was a beautiful cool morning, heavy with the salt air from the Irish Sea. We parked our rental car and carried our luggage into the ferry/bus terminal. It was quiet inside and there were few people since it was so early.

As the ferry from England docked, we could hear voices and see luggage-laden people walking through the terminal on their way to cars, taxis, or the bus. Among the crowd, we noticed a tired-looking, young mother carrying a toddler, with two bedraggled little blonde girls by her side. The girls appeared to be about 5 and 7 years old. Both wore tattered dresses that hung shapelessly from their thin bodies. The little family carried several pieces of battered, old luggage, which they placed in the corner by the door. The mother found a chair and sat tiredly with the toddler on her lap. The two little girls sat on the broken-down luggage close enough to touch their mother. Every few minutes, the mother would reach out a hand and gently brush the girls' hair from their faces.

My sister and I sat quietly sipping coffee, while our husbands relived some of the great moments from our trip to Ireland. We could see the older girl get up from her perch on the luggage, take the hand of her little sister, walk slowly over to the bakery counter, and look longingly at the buns and pastries; then she'd return to her mother's side. This happened several times. Finally, she grabbed her little sister's hand and walked once more to the bakery counter. This time she reached into her pocket and brought out coins. Almost defiantly, she handed the coins to the worker behind the counter, who counted them, shook her head, and handed them back to the little girl. Slowly, the child clutched her little sister's hand, and with her head down, she walked back to her mother's side.

I could not stand this any longer. I walked over to the mother and asked if they needed any help. "No," she said with a Celtic lilt, "we have missed the bus to Dublin, but another will be by this afternoon. We will wait." I walked back to my seat feeling terrible. I told the group waiting for me what the mother said. We all sat silently for a moment. Then, almost at the same time, we reached into our pockets and brought out handfuls of euros for which we no longer had any use.

I collected the euros and walked back to the mother. "We are leaving in a few minutes for England, and then we're going on to the United States. We have all these euros left over, and we will not be able to use them. Would you take them and perhaps get something for yourself and the girls?" She smiled shyly, nodded her head slightly, and I handed over the coins.

Before I got back to my chair, I noticed the older girl grab the hand of her little sister and *skip* to the bakery counter. We watched as she purchased three buns and three drinks, and put the leftover coins into her pocket. She carried her purchases proudly. On the way back to her mother, she went out of the way to walk in front of the four of us who sat quietly watching the little drama unfold. As she approached us, she looked directly into each of our eyes, held her head high, and gave us the joy-filled smile of a 7-year-old child, complete with a missing front tooth.

Our singular act of valuing this little family would not change their lives forever; but we knew that our action had made this day a better day. Making the most of this small moment in time had encouraged each of us. And, maybe, just like a pebble thrown into the water, which ripples all the way to the shore, this action would last longer than we expected and reach farther than we would ever know.

Last year I wrote *BRAVO Principal!*, which is about leadership and how principals build relationships that value others through their actions. Recently, when I told a teacher friend of mine that I was writing *BRAVO Teacher!*, she looked at me in surprise and said, "How are you going to do that?" Puzzled, I asked what she meant, and she responded, "You can't write a book like that for teachers. Teachers aren't leaders."

My friend was wrong. Of course, teachers are leaders, that is, when we choose to accept the leadership possibilities of teaching. There was a time when leadership in a school was considered to be vested in one person only, the principal. Although, it is true, that principals assume primary responsibilities for certain kinds of strategic leadership, such as bringing together the vision and aligning resources, in today's schools the concept of leadership is expanded to include teachers. Certainly, there is no doubt that teachers are leaders in instruction. Yet, while teacher leadership roles often vary from school to school and teacher to teacher, researchers have increasingly noted that teacher leadership is reflected in "establishing relationships, breaking down barriers, and marshalling resources throughout the organization in an effort to improve students' educational experiences" (York-Barr & Duke, 2004, p. 261).

Especially today, in this time of standardization and high-stakes assessment, teachers often are so constrained by rules, regulations, and testing that building relationships with students, parents, and co-workers seems less important and is easily forgotten. However, research is consistently reporting that what we have long known in our hearts is true: Positive relationships are at the very core of creating effective learning environments where all students achieve success (Bryk & Schneider, 2002). These relationships fostered by caring teachers and other adults, are critical to a child's "ability to grow up healthy and achieve later social, emotional, and academic success" (Ewing Marion Kauffman Foundation, 2002, p. 2). After all, why did we become teachers in the first place? We became teachers because we want to help children. Helping children begins when we make the most of every moment to establish strong, positive relationships.

How can teachers as leaders build the kind of valued relationships that strengthen schools? The key lies in building relationships that value all stakeholders: faculty, staff, students, parents, and the larger community. I call it BRAVO–Building Relationships with Actions that Value Others. BRAVO actions fall into seven categories:

1. Actions that uphold high standards for all children
2. Actions that empower
3. Actions that are respectful
4. Actions that are supportive
5. Actions that challenge the imagination
6. Actions that demonstrate culturally responsive teaching
7. Actions that are courageous

To illustrate the challenges that teachers face in building valuing relationships, I begin each chapter with a critical incident involving students from my own teaching experience. Their lives have stayed with me over the years, and the relationships that took place at that particular moment in time have reached farther than I ever thought possible. Today, after nearly 35 years as a teacher, my teaching continues to be guided by those relationships. Teachers have opportunities every day to build relationships with actions that value others. Many times, our singular actions of valuing do not change lives forever, nor are we always rewarded with a beatific smile, as we were in Ireland. But actions that value others create relationships (even if only for a moment) that change lives—a day at a time, a person at a time. Collectively, it is when we make the most of the moments we have with our students, that valuing actions lead to building lasting relationships, that change the world into a better place. And often this begins at school with teachers.

> The role of teacher remains the highest calling of a free people. To the teacher our nation entrusts her most precious resource, her children, and asks that they be prepared in all their glorious diversity to face the rigors of individual participation in a democratic society. (Shirley Hufstedler, Former U.S. Secretary of Education, Blaydes, 2003, p. 39)

1

Actions that Uphold High Standards— Point to the Stars

It is not a disgrace not to reach the stars, but it is a disgrace to have no stars to reach for.

Benjamin Mays

Grace Ann was my very first student. She was the first child to walk through the door of my fifth-grade classroom the very first year that I taught school, and she was smiling. She was tall, skinny, black, and poor. She lived in the nearby project, the oldest of nine children. Grace Ann was 12 years old. She was a good reader, although I don't remember ever seeing her select a book to read during free reading time. She said that she did not like math, but she was actually quite good with numbers when she chose to be. She loved kickball and was very good at it. Some days she would do her class work, and some days she would not. Some days she would bring in her homework, and some days she would not. Still, I liked having Grace Ann in my class. Even at 12, there was resilience about her—after all, she made it through each day still smiling.

One day I was visiting with the girls in our class at recess, and I asked them to tell me what they wanted to do when they grew up. Grace Ann responded first: "I want to sleep with lots of men, like my Mama does."

My first reaction was surprise—was she trying to shock me? Then, I looked clearly into her eyes. I did not see guile or sophisticated cleverness, instead I saw a child whose only goals quite simply were framed by the person she cared for the most—her mother.

The challenging question that all teachers face was set before me at that very moment: What could I do to point Grace Ann to the stars?

Grace Ann was my student in the days long before mandated standards and high-stakes testing, but the same challenge faces teachers today. How do we point our students to the stars? How do we uphold a high standard for every child? Here again, there are no easy answers. But the truth is, we have no choice. When we decided to become teachers, we committed to do all that we can to "[sustain] success for all students so that failure is not an option" (Blankstein, 2004, p. 5). This is not an easy task. But we know that most tasks worth doing are never easy. What could be more important than committing to make the world a better place by helping its future leaders?

State and national accountability standards and the No Child Left Behind Act of 2001 (NCLB) were created to help all children achieve, but there is no doubt that they are surrounded by controversy. Many educators support these standards because they feel that when applied properly they serve as specific criteria that guide schools with clear, consistent curriculum standards for all teachers to use for all children (Scheurich & Skrla, 2003). Yet, I hear teachers every day who are concerned that it may be harder today to uphold a high standard for every child because of the limits of these mandated accountability standards. Despite this complexity, teachers recognize that in the quest to uphold a high standard for every child, mandated high-stakes testing is a place to begin, not the place to end. BRAVO (Building Relationships with Actions that Value Others) teachers search their soul to understand themselves more fully and examine their own beliefs about children, they accept the responsibility to uphold a high standard for every child, and they create a classroom culture of achievement. When they do this, they build valuing relationships with all students that point them to the stars.

Search Your Soul

Before we can accept the responsibility to uphold high standards for every child, we must understand what we believe about ourselves as teachers and what we believe about children. When we glibly say that "every child can learn," do we really mean it, or have we just jumped on the bandwagon because it is politically correct to do so? These are deeply personal questions, but what we believe about ourselves as teachers, and what we believe about children, is a message that comes through loud and clear to our students, their parents, and other faculty. After examining our beliefs, we must evaluate our actions, then we must commit to taking the first step and doing what we believe, just as Rosa Parks did when she refused to go to the back of the bus. She said, "I knew someone had to take the first step, so I made up my mind, not to move" (Eisen, 1995).

Know Your Own Identity

Before you can understand the way that teachers influence the children in your classrooms, you must understand your own identity. Ask yourself the following questions (this is not a comprehensive list of identity questions, but it is a beginning):

- How do I describe myself?
- What is my family history?
- What is my purpose in life?
- What do I value?
- What kinds of careers are important to my family?
- What do I believe about gender roles?
- How do I relate to others?
- What do I believe about other people?
- Do I have friends who are from backgrounds different than mine?
- What do I do to enlarge my experiences with people of different cultures?

Now, ask yourself the following questions that specifically relate to teaching:

- What is the purpose of teaching?
- What do I believe about teaching children?
- What kind of behavior do I expect from students?
- What do I expect of my students' parents?
- Do I believe that every child can achieve?

When you reflect on these questions honestly and answer them privately, you will become aware of influences that perhaps you had no idea existed in your life and in your classroom. You will also understand why you relate better to some people than to others in some instances. Now, let's continue this journey to examine our beliefs and our actions.

Examine Your Beliefs

What you believe about yourself as a teacher and what you believe about all children are closely related. I don't want to sound trite, but consider this: What if you had been Helen Keller's teacher? Would you have believed in yourself and your abilities as a teacher enough to teach her? I know, I know, you are thinking you could not have been successful with someone with her deficits because you did not have the training. Well, you can't get off the hook that easily. Let's assume you have whatever training is necessary to work with any child. Would you have believed in yourself enough as a teacher to be able to teach Helen? You say, "Yes, I believe that I am an effective teacher, and effective teachers have the power to change children's lives."

Let's consider the next set of questions about what you believe about teaching: Do you believe that all children *want* to learn, regardless of their circumstances? Did Helen want to learn in spite of the dark, silent world in which she lived? You say, "Yes, she wanted to learn. Yes, I believe all children want to learn, regardless of their circumstances."

Now, take another step. Do you believe that all children can be successful or just some children? You say, "Yes, I believe that all children have the potential to be successful."

You have searched your soul and examined your beliefs, and here is what you believe: You believe in yourself as an effective teacher and you believe that effective teachers help children. You believe that all children want to learn regardless of their circumstances. You believe that all children have the potential to be successful.

Examine Your Actions

What do your actions say about what you believe? Do your actions show that you are always learning more about your craft so that you can be the most effective teacher possible? Or do you only attend professional development seminars when forced and then sit in the back row and grade your papers? I know some can be pretty boring—but that's not the point. The point is this: Do your actions show that you are so interested in learning more about teaching and about children that you take every opportunity to improve?

Because you believe that all children want to learn regardless of their circumstances, what do your actions show? Do you provide enrichment activities? Do you provide tutoring for children who are behind? Do you get to know all of your students so that you can understand what their needs are? Do you look for new, creative ways to motivate all of your children?

Because you believe that all children in your classroom have the potential to be successful, do you celebrate their successes? Do you celebrate individual improvement? Do you collaborate with parents to help them help you help their child? Do you team with other faculty to enhance learning opportunities for all children? You say, "Yes, yes, yes, yes, and yes, to all of these. My actions show that I believe in myself and in children."

Make a Personal Commitment

There is a story about a 5-year-old boy who had been cured of a life-threatening disease. Soon after, it was discovered that his sister had the same illness. Her only chance of recovery was a blood transfusion from him, because he had just the right antibodies. The doctor explained the situation to the little brother and asked if he would be willing to give his blood to his sister. He hesitated for only a moment before he said yes. As the transfusion progressed, he lay in bed next to his sister and smiled when he saw the color return to her cheeks. Then his face grew pale and his smile faded. He looked up at the doctor and asked, "Will I start to die right away?" Being young, the little boy had misunderstood the doctor and thought he had to give his sister all of his blood in order to save her. But he was willing to make a personal commitment to what he believed.

Now that you have explored your own beliefs and actions by looking deeply into your own soul, you need to make a personal commitment to uphold yourself to high standards and to hold every child that you teach to a high standard of achievement. In other words, you commit to doing what you say you believe. You commit to making the most of every moment you have with your students to point each of them to the stars.

Accept Responsibility to Uphold High Standards for Every Child

Now that we know that we believe in and are committed to holding ourselves and all of our students to a high standard of success, we are ready to accept this responsibility. To do this, it is important to look more closely at today's accountability system and high-stakes testing. Teachers must understand the dilemma created by high-stakes testing to commit to making standards work for all children.

Understand the Dilemma

I talk with teachers every day, and I have never met one who is not in favor of educator accountability. Just recently I was riding from the airport to my hotel with a woman who carried a bag with a big red apple on it. I asked if she was a teacher (silly question, I know). Of course, and she was on her way to a Texas Assessment of Knowledge and Skills (TAKS) conference. When I asked how she felt about all of the testing, she grimaced and said, "I am actually glad that we are being more accountable, ...but it seems that all we are allowed to do is teach to the test when there is so much more to teaching than testing!" Many teachers are frustrated and unhappy with the mandated accountability that is in place. Not because they are unwilling to be accountable, but because of the way it has been implemented. For example, consider the NCLB that requires that only 1% of children can be exempt from testing (now waived to 3%). Yet, in Texas, for example, the average number of identified special education students is 10% in a district. What about the other 7%? What do we do for them?

Unfortunately, many parents, and the media, do not understand the testing dilemma of standardized accountability. Certainly, accountability is appropriate and a good idea. But as James Popham (2005) points out, it is possible for schools labeled as "low performing" by NCLB tests to actually be doing a good job of instruction, especially considering that often these schools serve lower socioeconomic status (SES) students. At the same time, schools labeled as "high performing" might actually be doing a bad job of instruction since many of these schools serve students of higher socioeconomic status. In other words, sometimes, students in low SES schools have backgrounds that create barriers *when success is only determined by one test*, whereas high SES students tend to have the test-taking advantage and score well even though instruction has not been the best. The point of this comparison is not to question the quality of teachers in these schools, but to emphasize that the tests which are being used to determine teaching quality as they are written *do not measure teaching quality*. Success should be measured by considering a variety of factors including individual student improvement. These should be measured in a variety of ways that include portfolios and teacher observation.

Recently, I had a conversation with an excellent third-grade teacher whose class has made wonderful academic progress. However, at the beginning of the year, most of the students were below grade level, and the state test and NCLB designation of low or high performing will not be based on the individual gains of each child. Despite her good teaching and the children's achievement gains, it is likely their performance on the test will label the school as low performing. The problem is not holding children who are so different in so many ways to the same standard, but how we determine if that standard has been met. Testing all children in the same way, usually a multiple-choice test, is a one-size fits all mentality that does not consider the complexity, diversity, uniqueness, and individuality of children.

As high-stakes tests are implemented today, they are not always benchmarks to serve as a point of reference, instead they are often rigid where there should be a level of flexibility. Policymakers believe they are serving the best interests of our children, yet, they are relying on a simplistic answer to solve a very complex problem. It is our responsibility as teachers to understand the accountability dilemma and do what we can to influence its improvement.

We must have standards. A quick look at the achievement gap of children from different SES groups and from different racial groups makes it clear that we must provide academic standards for all children that serve as benchmarks. For example, since 1990 Caucasian students' scores on the National Assessment of Educational Progress (NAEP) math eighth-grade assessment have been an average of nearly 17% higher than African American scores and nearly 13% higher than Hispanic students (NCES, 2004). In reading and history the gap is somewhat less but still hovers around 10%; while in science Caucasian students score at least 20% higher. The same is true for the SAT and other tests (NCES, 2004). These data make it obvious that in the past too many educators have only believed that *some* children could be successful. But all of these children are the future leaders of our nation; clearly, it is in everyone's interest for *all* of our children to achieve at a high standard.

Make Standards Work

Scheurich and Skrla (2003) point out that the research shows that all schools that are highly successful "with all students *always* have clear, consistent curriculum standards that are known and used by all teachers" (p. 30). By benchmarking and aligning curriculum to the standards, schools take a critical step to ensure that standards work for students.

Recently, a school led by an award-winning principal failed to make adequate yearly progress (AYP) under NCLB guidelines, even though student achievement had steadily improved over several years (Carr, 2004). When the principal had taken over the school, scores were in the 40th percentile. Now, they were in the 70th percentile. But the school had not made its goal of 95% attendance. It had only achieved 94.5%.

The principal put a notice in the newspaper for the community to read that the school had failed to meet the AYP goal. She provided information that all achievement goals had been met, math and reading scores were up, but that the school had failed because of attendance. Parents were upset and did not want their children attending a school marked as a failure, but there was no other school nearby. Immediately, parents began contacting the school asking what they could do to help. Today, attendance is higher than the required 95%. Additionally, this wise principal with the support of faculty members accomplished three goals with this one action: understanding of the problem of high-stakes testing and standardized goals improved among the community, parents shared with the school in the responsibility for fixing the failure, and school attendance improved.

Building positive relationships with students influences their school attendance and how hard they work at difficult school tasks (Bryk & Driscoll, 1998), which in turn helps students achieve higher standards. So, the very act of building strong relationships and holding all children to a high standard helps them meet that standard.

Standardized accountability isn't going away. I expect it to be around for a long time. Educators must accept responsibility for upholding standards, even if we don't agree with the way they are being implemented at the moment. Even more, we must accept the responsibility to uphold high standards for every child that goes beyond state and national requirements. Once we understand the dilemma, we must make standards work for the benefit of all our students.

Calm High-Stakes Test Fears

I was watching television in Houston, Texas, the night before the TAKS high-stakes tests were to be given throughout the state. I will never forget what I saw. The television reporter stood with a mother and a little boy who was probably about seven. She held up the microphone and asked the child how he felt about the tests tomorrow. This little boy began to describe his fears—He was afraid he would fail the test and repeat the grade, get sick while taking the test, wouldn't sleep that night, his teachers would be mad at him if he did poorly, and fail the test, but that his friends would pass. Visibly holding back tears, he listed a few other fears. Should a test cause a 7-year-old boy to have that many fears? Should one test decide whether a student passes to the next grade level?

At about the same time, the *San Antonio Express-News* printed a story detailing the story of a senior girl who had taken all of her course work and passed all of her classes, but she was unable to pass the TAKS test, even though she had taken the multiple-choice test on several occasions, plus participated in tutoring classes offered by her school. Because of this, she would not graduate with her class, nor would she be able to accept the scholarship that a local university had offered her!

I don't know what the probabilities are for students who fail the high-stakes TAKS test the first time to pass it on the next try. But I know that for law students who fail the Texas bar exam on the first attempt, their chances of failing it a second time increase, rather than decrease, often as a result of increased test anxiety!

The high-stakes test fears do not stop with students; teachers and principals are fearful, too, as they share in the condemnation if their students do not do well on the exam. But, of course, everyone is feeling the heat. Principals are called on the carpet by superintendents who are under pressure from the school board to get the coveted Exemplary District rating that Texas schools can earn if the test scores are high enough. Some schools have even resorted to cheating so that their schools won't be labeled as a failing school.

A school principal noted that she had been hired at her school to raise the level of performance on statewide assessments (Harris, 2005). Giving in to this pressure she now feels that she actually added to student anxieties by reminding struggling children of the consequences of failing the test and constantly stressing the importance of the test. She also feels that her concern translated to teachers as a lack of trust in their abilities.

There is no way that teachers can *force* children to pass high-stakes tests. But we can put our energies into focusing on improvement and achievement, rather than testing. As we recognize children for improving, they will be enabled to achieve more. Even though the tests are hugely important, in our classrooms we must de-emphasize the test itself. As students increase their confidence in themselves and in their abilities to achieve, tension and fears will lessen and they will test better.

Teachers tell me that when they focus more on the whole child and less on the test, their classrooms become more student centered. They acknowledge that they must prepare students for the exams and expectations remain high, but in the words of one teacher, "when we balance this with an emphasis on praise and encouragement for great efforts, we become calmer with the students and the results are better all around."

Uphold High Standards with Actions That Create a Culture of Achievement

Accepting that accountability is here to stay, BRAVO teachers must create classroom cultures of achievement. This means that high standards for every child should be incremental, focus on individual expectations, and be integrated throughout the curriculum.

Consider Standards as Incremental

The students in our classrooms are at different stages of growth. Every child *can* learn, but they learn at different paces and in different ways, or as the saying goes: Every child can learn, but not always on the same day the same way. Some are doing their very best, some are not making any visible progress at all, and others fall somewhere between those extremes at any given time. Some are ready to read when they come to school, some are not. Some are ready for Algebra in the seventh grade, some are not. Some are ready for calculus as juniors, some are not (I'm still not ready!). If a kindergartner is not ready to read at the age of 5, that doesn't mean that she will not learn to read. It means that if she is not *yet* ready to read; teachers must provide the structure and support necessary to increase her readiness. Teachers must be proactive. This is why it is so important for educators to consider standards incrementally. By this I mean that standards should be considered in three stages: good, better, and best. St. Francis said it this way: "Start by doing what's necessary, then do what's possible, and suddenly you are doing the impossible" (Blaydes, 2003, p. 81). It's not about getting more, but becoming more.

Believing that all children can achieve high standards, our first goal is that they achieve a minimum or good standard. But learning should not stop there, and this is where it gets messy. In a test environment such as we have today, when so many decisions for children, teachers, and schools are based on the test results, the tendency is to teach to the test. This is happening all over the United States as teachers tell me that they no longer are allowed to take classes on field trips, participate in special programs, or other enhancing activities. Instead, many are limited to drills and test reviews in preparation for the all-important tests. Consequently, when everyone passes the test at the required score, the tendency is to say that we have reached our goal, the standards have been met.

Focus on High Expectations

Once reached, standards are never a place to stop, instead they are a place to start anew to achieve higher standards. When students achieve the minimum or good standard, this should be celebrated. Then we work to motivate our students to be *better*. Then, having achieved *better*, we encourage them to reach the *best*. Teachers must establish this climate of achievement on an individual basis because different students will be at different levels of achievement. The differentiated classroom at work! Teachers who know their students are able to discern student readiness for the next standard.

Teacher expectations are keys to creating a culture of achievement. I'm reminded of a poem that emphasized the importance of expectations. According to the poem there was a pretty good school where a pretty good student sat in a pretty good class taught by a pretty good teacher who always accepted pretty good work for students to pass. It goes on to say that even though the student wasn't great at anything he was pretty good and that was okay. It wasn't until the student went to look for a job that he began to realize that pretty good might not be good enough. Teachers should celebrate a student's achievement of pretty good, but the expectations for achievement must not stop there. Michelangelo said, "The greatest danger for most of us is not that our aim is too high and we will miss it, but that it is too low and we will reach it" (Blaydes, p. 137).

Teachers have opportunities every day to encourage student expectations. We verbalize high expectations of our students in many ways throughout the day. We ask a student to continue working on a paper because we know the student can do better. We don't accept work that we can't read. We help a child find a library book that is doable but a challenge. We encourage and inspire a high standard when we remind students that "I know you can do this," or when we note on a creative writing assignment, "You are a good writer. I enjoyed this."

We increase expectations in a student's ability, which leads to higher standards when we increase responsibility. Shane was a junior in a small high school that shared a campus with all grade levels from 1 to 12. He was a minimal student, had a short temper, was often rude to other students his age, and was often in trouble for talking back to teachers. One teacher referred to him as a "bull in a china closet." One day a teacher observed him getting off the school bus with an elementary student, and as they parted, she heard the younger student thank him. The next day she noticed the same thing. She went to the elementary student and asked why he was thanking Shane. The child said, "Oh, he listens to me read my stories on the bus." To make a long story short, Shane was invited to help with the school's new tutorial program, which paired high school students with elementary students who needed extra help. The change in his behavior was almost immediate. At the end of the year when the students evaluated the program, Shane wrote that he thought he would go to college after all, because he would be a good teacher. Expectations lead to upholding higher standards for individual students! Expectations tell students that we believe in them and know they can achieve more.

Integrate Expectation
Throughout the Curriculum

The expectation of achievement should be integrated throughout the curriculum—the test should not be the curriculum. Now you take a test. Which teacher is integrating high expectations throughout the curriculum, Teacher A or Teacher B?

Teacher A: Bob believes that knowledge is assessed by achieving the right answers to questions on the test. Lesson plans are coordinated with state curriculum guides. As the teacher, he does not need to explain why these are the right answers, it is enough to know that this is what the experts have learned and we should learn from the experts, although he does patiently point out where the correct answers are in the test. The syllabus for the class consists of mastering each objective as outlined in the state curriculum guide for the subject being taught. Students are prepared for the high-stakes test with practice and drill.

Teacher B: Bill loves the class that he is teaching. He is eager to share information and engage the students in dialogue about the topic. Students prepare projects utilizing a variety of media and present these to the class. Bill is careful to help the students relate the topic they are presenting with experiences from their own lives. In the process, the students identify objectives outlined in the state curriculum guide and relate these objectives to their presentation. Students have fun preparing for the high-stakes tests and master the content under the direction of their teacher.

Which teacher, A or B, is integrating high expectation standards throughout the curriculum? You selected Teacher B? Congratulations, you are right! I knew you could do it! When teachers integrate a high expectation of learning throughout the curriculum, the standard becomes higher for all—teachers and students.

I have a friend who tells this story about her 9-year-old son. It seems that she was always telling him that he couldn't have everything he wanted, and she invariably ended this little speech with, "Even if you had it, you wouldn't want it, after all." One time they stayed at a really fancy hotel for a night. When he walked in and looked around at the beautiful lobby, he was just in awe. Finally, he turned to his mother and said, "Tell me again why rich people aren't happy?" We tell our students and our own children that in life one just can't have it all. But this is not true about upholding high standards. When our actions uphold high standards for all students, we increase their chances to have it all.

Tactical Actions That Uphold High Standards

What tactical actions upholding high standards can teachers implement that build relationships that value others?

- Understand what you believe.
- Assess your actions to match your beliefs.
- Acknowledge responsibility to hold every child to a high standard.
- Communicate that all students are held accountable to achieve.
- Provide enrichment activities for all students.
- Provide tutorial support for all students.
- Build on standards that are incremental.
- Reflect on where the student is in his growth.
- Create a plan for the student to improve.
- Acknowledge improvement.
- Verbalize the need to move to higher standards.
- Calm test fears in the classroom.
- De-emphasize the test, emphasize improvement.
- Build student confidence.
- Expect great things from students.
- Be specific about expectations.
- Plan lesson plans with high expectations integrated throughout learning objectives.

Our students need to be challenged with high expectations that are tailored for each child. BRAVO teachers uphold high expectations when they have relationships that are strong and that value each child as an individual. High-stakes assessment standards when not integrated throughout the curriculum with student needs in mind—are like a hammer. When we make the most of each moment and search our soul to know what we believe, accept the responsibility of upholding high standards for all children, and create a culture of achievement in our classrooms, high standards become the telescope for students to find their star. As a teacher, I could not change the home circumstances of Grace Ann's life. But I could give her a telescope.

Remember, BRAVO teachers build relationships that value others by upholding high standards for all children.

Actions That Uphold High Standards
Point to the Stars

Search Your Soul

- Know Your Own identity
- Examine Your Beliefs
- Examine Your Actions
- Make a Personal Commitment to Uphold High Standards for Every Child

Accept Responsibility

- Understand the Dilemma
- Make Standards Work
- Calm High-Stakes Test Fears

Uphold High-Standards with Actions That Create a Culture of Achievement

- Consider Standards as Incremental
- Focus on High Expectations
- Integrate Expectation Throughout the Curriculum

2

Actions That
Are Empowering—
Less Is More

My willingness to be less made her more.

Noah benShea

"It's Le tee cee a, not Letisha!" Leticia corrected me, very importantly. Petite and pretty with flashing dark, brown eyes, Leticia (pronounce it correctly) was in my remedial reading class with three other first graders. She was new to the class, and the year was almost over. One of the first-grade teachers had told me about Leticia. She had completed the whole set of first-grade readers with her class, but she still could not read a word.

Even though there was not much time left in the school year, I suggested that the teacher let Leticia come to my reading class for an hour each day. I had a group of students who were struggling in a beginning reader, and she would probably fit with them very nicely. So every day Leticia came to our reading class, eager to learn to read. She sounded out every word laboriously. She listened when the other students read. She hung on every word I said. She wanted desperately to learn to read.

Leticia made steady progress in our resource reading class. One day after reading an entire page aloud without a mistake, Leticia looked up from her book, flashed a brilliant smile, and yelled exuberantly for all the class to hear, "Wow! Listen to me. I can read!" That was more than 30 years ago, and I still vividly remember the moment that Leticia learned to read. It was also the moment that I saw in action a teacher's ability to empower. What a feeling for both of us!

Generally, we read about empowerment in schools in the context of site-based councils *if* the principal decides (or is mandated) to share power to involve faculty and others in various aspects of the school, such as budgeting, for example. Yet, another aspect of empowerment occurs when principals share or give away some of their power to teachers to create a positive school climate (Matthews & Crow, 2003).

Still, another perspective of empowerment is the notion that the leader chooses to use power less so that others can use their power more. In so doing, the leader actually becomes more influential (powerful), because the participation of others creates a buy-in that might not have been possible before; in other words, less is more. This was supported when I surveyed more than 100 teachers about what good principals do to promote a positive school climate that emphasizes teacher quality and student learning. Each teacher pointed out how important it was to be empowered (Harris, 2000). When principals empower teachers by using less of their power, this often leads to teachers using less of their power so that students become empowered. This cycle of becoming less so that others become more contributes to a positive school climate and builds teacher/student relationships that encourage students to act maturely, cooperate more successfully with others, and develop their talents more fully (Booth, 1997).

Teacher instructional leadership is a powerful way that teachers empower students as evidenced in Leticia's joy. But today's enhanced view of leadership potential promotes a sense of a teacher's own empowerment, transcends instruction, and leads to empowering others through actions that build leadership capacity, encourage authentic learning, and demonstrate democratic principles. These kinds of empowering actions build relationships that value students and others.

Empowering Others Through Actions That Build Leadership Capacity

Leadership capacity refers to "broad-based, skillful participation in the work of leadership" (Lambert, 2003, p. 4). In other words, there are opportunities throughout an organization for many people to engage in leadership. Leadership exists at every level: Principals can be leaders, teachers can be leaders, students can be leaders, and parents can be leaders. But it is teacher leadership that "is at the heart of the high leadership capacity school" (Lambert, p. 32). When schools have a high level of leadership involvement it is likely that the school will have a high level of achievement. Empowering actions that build relationships through valuing others to sustain leadership capacity include sharing the vision, collaborating, and reflecting.

Share in the Vision

The principal is usually charged with the role of communicating the school vision; however, if teachers do not share the same vision and communicate its goals through their teaching, the vision becomes meaningless. In fact, when teachers were asked what they considered the single most important act their principal did, one out of four reported that it was empowering them to share in identifying and clarifying the school vision (Harris, 2000). Being a part of creating the school vision encourages buy-in; after all, it's hard to not participate in something that we helped create.

Sharing in the vision of the school means that as teachers we model that vision in all that we do. When teachers commit to a shared vision everything that is done at school whether it is teaching delivery, curriculum design, or classroom management is filtered through the school's shared vision. For example, when Rosa Smith, an Ohio educator, read that 75% of the United States prison population is Latino or African American and 80% are functionally illiterate, her vision for schools changed from teaching math or science, to saving lives (Blankstein, 2004)! It is our vision that keeps our purpose clear, constantly reminding us that we should always be doing what is best for our students. A school's vision hanging on a wall in the classroom for all to read that says "Every child can learn" means nothing if the meaning and intent are not brought to life in what happens at school. Abraham Maslow said, "If we don't model what we teach, we are teaching something else" (Blaydes, p. 26). It is the same with our vision—it should guide what and how we teach.

Collaborate

Roland Barth said, "To perform like a team, act like a team—together" (Barth, 2003, p. 59). There is strength in togetherness that empowers each of us as team members. Participating in active collaboration with other teachers, parents, and students unleashes ideas we might never have thought of on our own. Collaboration also encourages a feeling of responsibility for the school and its activities. When teachers have the opportunity to collaborate and work as a team with teachers at other grade levels, we begin to see the curriculum in a much broader scope. We understand the necessity to accomplish certain tasks because we see more clearly how one knowledge set builds on another. As one kindergarten teacher said, "When I began this work as a teacher leader, I saw myself as a kindergarten teacher. Now I see myself as an educator" (Lambert, 2003, p. 7).

Many times I was absolutely at my wit's end with students who would not complete work or obey our classroom rules. Invariably, when I brought my problems to our faculty team meetings, another teacher would have additional information about the child or the situation and we would collaboratively find alternative strategies that could work. Other times, I invited parents to team with me to share their suggestions.

I remember one of the first times that I collaborated with parents about a behavior problem. John had a history of petty misbehaviors at school, and previous teachers complained that there was no parent support at all. On the advice of another teacher, I invited the parents to join me in developing a behavior management plan. They came to the classroom almost defiantly. I had arranged three chairs in a sort of circle, and when they entered the room, I invited them to sit with me. We began to talk, and when it became clear that they really had been invited to help me help John, we began to collaborate on strategies that might work. It took more than one meeting, but John's behavior improved that year. The parents made progress also and began to see that they could partner with the school to help, rather than be blamed for having a "bad kid." (This is how the Dad referred to his son at that first meeting.) I made progress, too, as I learned the strength of collaboration as an empowering tool that sustained leadership capacity. This valuing action of parents and teachers working together as a team enhances relationships and strengthens schools.

Reflect

To teach without reflecting is like reading a book and not understanding a word of it. As teachers, we build leadership capacity when we take time to reflect on what happens at school. Reflective teachers are not content to teach lessons, instead they are always considering "the evidence surrounding themselves—the day-to-day behavior of their students as they go about learning and growing" (Pang, 2005, p. 252). This is an empowering cycle that builds relationships through insightful valuing of our experiences. It looks like this:

Reflection → Critical self inspection → Self correction → Reflection
(Harris & Lowery, 2003, p. xv)

Reflection causes us to ponder, consider, and rethink our own actions and experiences that have occurred during the day. Critical inspection is when we find ourselves thinking "I wonder what would have happened if I had done this—or this?" This leads to self-correction, which means that we commit right now to deal with the situation in a different way. Once we self-correct, then the cycle continues. Getting in the habit of reflection and *making* time to do this is not only empowering but leads to a constant cycle of ongoing improvement by building our leadership capacity. At the same time that reflective practice encourages self dialogue, it also builds relationships with faculty, students, and parents as we all begin to participate in the dialogue of improvement, which reflective practice encourages.

Empowering Others Through Authentic Learning

Jerry Starratt, a professor at Boston College, spoke at a Phi Delta Kappa meeting at my university in November 2004. His theme challenged educators to commit to authentic learning, and to do all that we can to help students understand the natural, social, and cultural worlds where they live. At the same time, authentic learning should result in helping students find themselves in their learning encounters. When this happens, learners are empowered to not only know more about who they are, but also to understand more about who they want to become. To emphasize authentic learning, teachers must make the most of teaching moments to incorporate principles into their relationships with students that include nurturing learning that builds on student experiences, emphasizing connections between facts and ideas, and acknowledging that students are multidimensional.

Build on Student Experiences

Students are not empty vessels, and teachers do not know it all! I have been an educator for nearly 35 years, and I still have to remind myself of this. When I prepare for a class, whether teaching first graders (years ago) or teaching doctoral students at the university (which I do today), I still have to consciously stop myself from *telling* my students everything that I know about the topic. When I begin the class by asking students what they know about a specific topic, I am amazed at how often the ensuing dialogue covers much of what I had been prepared to tell them! The author John Steinbeck (1955) noted that he had three outstanding teachers in his life, and "they did not tell—they catalyzed a burning desire to know." Teaching is not about telling. Teaching is about inspiring others to learn more. William Arthur Ward wrote, "The mediocre teacher tells. The good teacher explains. The superior teacher demonstrates. The great teacher inspires" (Blaydes, 2003, p. 35). Still the most common form of instructional delivery used by teachers today is lecture—another word for *telling*. Often we teachers are so busy telling students what we think they should know that their rich life experiences remain known only to them.

Teaching concepts by building on student experiences not only brings authenticity to the learning, it empowers students to participate actively and understand their own self-worth. I assigned a book report for my fifth graders. We went to the library, and one of the boys who was a poor reader wanted to check out *The Call of the Wild* by Jack London. The librarian and I discouraged him, knowing that it would be too challenging, and he would become frustrated. However, two weeks later he presented his book report to the class. Then he checked out *White Fang*, followed by every other dog book that he could find. What had happened? He had been given a dog for Christmas and, for the first time, connected a school assignment with something that he truly cared about. Authentic learning!

When student experiences are acknowledged with respect, their very existence is validated; and it doesn't matter how old the student is. I remember sitting in my first class as a 40-year-old doctoral student. The class was debating school choice. None of the students had any particular experience with school choice, but I did. I had been a teacher and administrator in public and private schools. Still nervous when I spoke in class, my hands were sweating, my heart raced, and my mouth was dry—but I raised my hand and shared some of my experiences. When I finished, Dr. Scribner, my professor, said something positive about my comments, and the discussion continued. I still remember the pride I felt when my experience contributed to the lesson conversation.

Even Socrates acknowledged that knowledge was already in his students, and he just had to unlock that key. In this way, teachers empower students through authentic learning when we use case studies, dialogue, simulations, role playing, and much more. Instead of being told about the Civil War, for example, authentic learning brings that historic conflict alive when teachers connect it to the experiences of a child who has a parent in the military. Authentic learning that empowers students builds on their life experiences to create new learning and new understandings. At the same time, it contributes to a classroom environment that fosters relationships that value others.

Connect Facts to Ideas

Most teachers have a tendency to ask questions that require specific answers rather than those which explore ideas. If it were up to most of us, we might even say, bring on the workbooks! (Well, maybe we wouldn't, but we would be sorely tempted!) After all, it is so easy to grade a worksheet with answers that are either right or wrong. Who has time to read a long essay question response—especially with some of our large classes? And, to make it worse, most of the high-stakes tests that matter today are multiple-choice tests with right or wrong answers and no room for conjecture or exploring ideas. Motivational speaker Hanoch McCarty noted that "Socrates didn't have an overhead projector. He asked questions that bothered people and 3,500 years after people are still talking about him" (Blaydes, 2003, p. 28).

When facts are presented in isolation, learning is limited. When facts become the bridge to larger ideas and concepts that cause students to question and seek further, then learning becomes authentic and dynamic. There was a time as an elementary teacher that I had students copy spelling words over and over again. Then one day it suddenly dawned on me that copying the words, even knowing how to spell them, had no relationship at all to understanding the words and being able to use them to communicate ideas. Instead, I began asking students to write sentences and stories sharing their ideas by using their spelling words. The students enjoyed this more, learned more, and I learned much more about my students. It's like the concept of *pi*. I know it has value of approximately 3.14 and goes on to infinity. But I have absolutely no understanding of why that is important or what part it plays in physics or algebra (or is it geometry?). I know what it *is,* but what *does* it mean? We empower students with authentic learning when we make the most of teaching moments to take isolated facts and relate them to ideas that build a bridge of knowledge to use tomorrow. The author Graham Greene described this as that moment "in a child's life when the door opens and lets the future in" (Blaydes, 2003, p. 53).

Another way that teachers empower students by building a bridge to the future with authentic learning is to share their own enthusiasm for learning. I know a high school teacher who once said that he sometimes got so excited when he was teaching that he would get chills. His students told me that it was fun to be in his classroom because he got so excited about what he was teaching that they couldn't help but get excited, too! Another teacher said, "I'm really a bit of an actress, when I introduce a new topic to the class I act like it's one of my favorite things to teach. The kids get excited, and, you know, so do I!"

Acknowledge That Students Are Multidimensional

I am a daughter, a sister, a wife, a mother, a friend, a teacher, a writer, a blonde (well, sort of!). In each of these settings, a different dimension of me becomes evident. In some settings I am quiet, and in others, I am animated. Some who know me say I have a great sense of humor; others think I am too serious. Our students are like this, too. While we know them as students, they are also sons, daughters, brothers, sisters, athletes, musicians, boyfriends, girlfriends, and much, much more.

Many of our students have talents that we never glimpse in school. I remember Tim, who was a senior, but in trouble most of the time. None of his teachers could motivate him; his grades were so poor that we were afraid he would not graduate with his class. Then one day Tim's advisor teacher just happened to be visiting a new church in the community. At the beginning of the service, a young man walked on stage and played a violin solo so beautifully that it brought tears to the teacher's eyes. That violinist was Tim. When the amazed teacher went back to school that week, he shared this dimension of the troublesome student with other teachers. As teachers acknowledged this aspect of Tim, they began to see him differently and work with him more effectively. Although Tim could still be difficult, his grades and his behavior began to improve, and he graduated with his class that year.

When we stand at the front of our classrooms and look at our students, we must remember that they are far more than students. They have hopes, dreams, and discouragements that we may never know. If our actions do not value all students, we limit what they will become. A student's picture of himself is often a reflection of what teachers think of him. What a child thinks he is, he is most likely to become. We empower our students when we recognize their multiple dimensions of self as multilayers of valuable personhood. Actions that empower students through authentic learning build relationships that demonstrate not only how much we value them but how much they value themselves.

Empowering Others with Actions That Demonstrate Democratic Principles

A major purpose of education is to prepare young people to become leaders in a democratic society. How do we do this as teachers? How will this lead to building relationships? John Dewey (1937) pointed out that democracy is "faith in human intelligence" (p. 458); it extends "the basic freedom" to choose ways to produce this intelligence (p. 459); and it invites "participation for the good of all its members on equal terms" (Dewey, 1916, p. 105). In other words, democracy is an empowering action. We empower students, teachers, parents, and other stakeholders with democratic actions that demonstrate faith in their abilities, extend opportunities to choose, and invite participation.

Demonstrate Trust

The concept of democracy resonates with a belief in the goodness and talents of people. We demonstrate this belief in others by trusting them. We demonstrate this trust in our students when we act on the belief that every child can learn. Teachers who have little trust in students, co-workers, or others are not able to empower anyone. The very act of empowering says "I trust you enough to share my power, so that you can become more; I believe in you." When we trust others we are able to delegate responsibility, which builds collegial relationships with co-workers and gives students freedom to participate more fully in their own education.

In one of my first years of teaching, I was a remedial reading specialist in a pull-out program. Timothy was in the second grade, and because he was very behind in reading, he came to my class every day for an hour for individual tutoring. In that setting, with resource help every day, Timothy's reading progressed at a rapid pace. He was very proud of this new ability and boasted that he could read as well as anyone else in second grade (which was not quite true; not yet, anyway).

One day as I walked by Timothy's classroom, his teacher beckoned me to come into the room. She was standing at Timothy's desk with a reading book in her hand. Timothy sat at his desk, his shoulders hunched over the reader. To my shock, I heard her say, "Now, Timothy, show her that you *can't* read." And he couldn't. He sat in his chair, never taking his eyes off the book—and he could not read a word, not one! I remember just standing there, my mind racing to say or do something but not knowing what. Finally, I said, "Well, he reads just fine for me" and left the room. The next day when he came to reading class, he read very nicely; but he could not read for someone who did not trust in his ability to read.

We also demonstrate our trust in others when we allow ourselves as teachers to become vulnerable enough to share our inner selves. I was reading *Old Yeller* aloud to my third-grade class and I was at the part where the old hound dies. I could hardly read because I was trying so hard to keep from crying in front of the students. I glanced up from the book to see some of the children trying desperately not to cry, and big tears were forming in the eyes of others. I closed the book, and we all cried. Sharing our emotions that day was a visible action that increased the connection of students and teacher and strengthened us as a community of learners.

A trusting faith in the possible waits quietly within our students until it is empowered to become reality. Noah benShea (2003) said it this way, "Faith's challenge is not to believe that we will get more, but become more" (p. 125). We empower students to believe in themselves and become more, but not until they trust that we believe in them.

Provide Choice

An important principle in democratic learning is empowering people to choose. However, in most of our classrooms there is rarely opportunity for children to choose. Instead, we create assignments and expect all of our students to respond appropriately. Yet providing opportunities for choice is an important quality of democracy and one that communicates a sense of empowerment through expressed freedom. When we trust our students and believe in them, we demonstrate this by giving them opportunities to choose to participate in different ways in their own learning.

I learned a valuable lesson in my first year of teaching about the importance of choice. It was so simple, I almost missed it. Each day I listed on the chalkboard five or six different activities for my fourth graders that included a mix of reading, writing, and drawing, with the most important assignments as number 1 and 2. The more fun activities were usually numbered 5 or 6. Although some of the students completed everything every day, there were several who never got beyond assignment 2 or 3. I shared my frustration with an experienced teacher and she gave a very simple suggestion. The next day I again listed five or six reinforcement activities on the board. When the students came to class, I said: "Everyone must do activities 1 and 2; then you may do 3, 4, 5, and 6 in any order you choose." The next day, I said: "Everyone must do assignments 1 and 2. Then you may do any three of the other four activities; it's your choice." This simple act of choice, giving students the freedom to choose which activities to do made a huge difference. Soon, everyone in the room was energized and working diligently at what they had *chosen* to do.

I'm reminded of a high school history teacher who decided to demonstrate democracy in the classroom. At the end of a unit on U.S. presidents, she asked students to choose their own assessment project. One young man, who rarely spoke in class and just barely passed the pencil-and-paper tests, chose to create a video of the president (I think it was Woodrow Wilson) giving a speech at a campaign rally. He even designed a campaign button and wrote a campaign song.

When the teacher shared this with me, she could not keep the excitement from her voice and kept saying, "I had no idea he was so talented!"—all because she gave him voice in an opportunity to demonstrate his talents. Demonstrating democratic principles through choice can lead to new understandings that result in greater valuing of others.

Invite Participation

Democratic actions invite participation from everyone in the class. This means that as teachers we must be sensitive, alert, and observant. Are the same students participating in everything, while other students sit passively uninvolved?

Unfortunately, this is probably so. For example, female teachers have a tendency to call on boys more than girls. We rarely call on students if we think they will not know the answer. Nor do we take the time to prepare these children to respond to a question that they can answer. Are we still letting children choose team members—when we know that certain children will always be chosen first, and others will always be last? What are we doing to make sure that in our classrooms *every child has an equal opportunity to fully participate?*

A master teacher I know created class lists and checked off names of students she called on or asked to do special things for her. In this way, she could tell if she was inviting participation of the same students or if she was equitably involving everyone.

What are we doing to involve parents? Or once again, are we involving the very same parents all the time without reaching out to others? Many times, all it takes to extend participation is an invitation—a note, a phone call, or an e-mail. When we contact parents and personally invite them to participate in some way, most are pleased and eager to help. Over the years, I often received notes saying, "I work, but I want to help, please call on me when you need something." Notice the pride on a student's face when their parent comes to school to help or volunteer in some way.

Another way that we empower others through democratic participation is to simply acknowledge them. Over the years, students have often told me that just having a teacher who calls them by name makes them feel valued. A high school student wrote the following comment on a teacher evaluation:

> I don't like being called "Sweetie." She's not fooling me. I know that means that I'm not important enough for her to know my name.

After being a K–12 teacher and administrator for nearly 30 years, I took a position with a university. All of a sudden I was in a completely different environment and, at the bottom of the university hierarchy, a junior assistant professor. That summer I attended a large national conference where I did not know anyone well, although I had been introduced to a few professors at an earlier meeting. On this particular day, I walked into a huge room full of people talking and laughing with one another. Immediately, I felt uncomfortable. Should I look for a familiar face? Should I try to find an empty table? I had just decided to leave, when I heard someone call my name. I looked up to see Dr. John Hoyle, a well-known university professor, standing in the center of the room at a table with friends. He called my name again and motioned for me to come join them. I couldn't believe he had remembered my name or even recognized me. But he had and I have never forgotten the importance of being acknowledged and how empowered I felt.

Tactical Actions That Empower

A friend of mine, Dr. Charlie Blanton, has been teaching leadership for many years. He often prefaces his statements with "Now this is what my teacher told me. . . ." One day, when we were visiting, he said, "My teacher told me to never use the word 'activities', but to use 'tactics' instead. Activities are often directionless and become busywork; the word 'tactics' implies purposeful intent." What tactical actions can BRAVO (Building Relationships with Actions that Value Others) teachers implement that build relationships which value others through empowerment?

- ♦ Increase opportunities for student responsibility (beyond cleaning out the fish tank!).
- ♦ Provide opportunities for leadership among students.
- ♦ Collaborate with parents.
- ♦ Ask students, other faculty, and parents for input in classroom decisions.
- ♦ Give students choices in the classroom.
- ♦ Involve students and parents in evaluating assignments.

- Participate in committees that are creating a vision statement.
- Develop a plan for implementing the school's vision in your classroom.
- Share your ideas for modifying the school vision when necessary.
- Create a classroom vision statement that aligns with the school vision.
- *Make* time to reflect on your actions each day.
- Keep a journal.
- Provide opportunities for students to talk about their experiences.
- Plan classroom lessons around student experiences.
- Integrate the higher-order thinking skills.
- Ask open-ended questions.
- Know students' interests.
- Address students by their name.
- Know faculty members' interests.

BRAVO teachers make the most of every moment to empower others when they build leadership capacity at every level, emphasize authentic learning, and demonstrate democratic principles on the school campus. John Denver, the singer-songwriter, wrote that "We are the dwelling place of incredible opportunities. They live within us" (Blaydes, p. 20). Actions that are empowering build relationships that value others as our less becomes their more. Just ask Leticia.

Remember, BRAVO teachers build relationships with actions that value others through empowering them.

Actions That Are Empowering

Less Is More

Empowering Others Through Actions That Build Leadership Capacity

- Share in the Vision
- Collaborate
- Reflect

Empower Others Through Authentic Learning.

- Build on Student Experiences
- Connect Facts to Ideas
- Acknowledge That Students Are Multidimensional

Empower Others with Actions That Demonstrate Democratic Principles.

- Demonstrate Trust
- Provide Choice
- Invite Participation

3

Actions That Demonstrate Respect for All— Every Individual Is Important

Respect for the fragility and importance of an individual life is still the mark of an educated man.

Norman Cousins

Actions
That Demonstrate
Respect for All—
Every Individual
Is Important

Jason was a fifth grader—one of those kids who just didn't fit in with any group. He looked different from the other children in the classroom. His brown hair covered his head in tight ringlets, and his complexion was pale with red-brown freckles that splashed across his face as if from a careless paint brush. He was tall and skinny, and he wore clothes that were two sizes too big. His voice was soft; his hands were delicate and always in motion. Jason wouldn't play sports, because he was afraid of the ball. He didn't like to run, because he "didn't like to sweat." Jason knew that he was different from his classmates, and after several unsuccessful attempts to join in, he isolated himself from the other students. He did not belong and he knew it.

But Jason could write. Even his spelling sentences, which most fifth graders churned out with boring regularity, were fascinating to read. I eagerly looked forward to creative writing papers because Jason could bring to almost any story a twist of imagination that was always surprising. He was a talented young man, with a delightful sense of humor—on paper.

I tried to build Jason's confidence through his writing and to boost his status in the classroom. But his talent just could not compete with basketball and football among the other fifth graders. At recess he would visit with me, or stand off to the side of the playground watching the other children. Often he brought his notebook outside, and I would see him standing or sitting alone, his pencil moving on the paper, oblivious to the childish activity around him.

Just before the school year was over, Jason moved out of the state. His last day in my classroom, he left a note on my desk that simply said:

Thank you for being my friend and teaching me.

                              With Respect,
                              Jason

I cried when I saw the note that Jason left on my desk. Had I done everything that I could to foster a sense of belonging in our classroom for Jason? Had I done everything that I could to help him find a friend? Had my actions toward him demonstrated my respect for him as a person? In the years that have followed, Jason's note "with respect" has silently challenged me to do all that I can to achieve a respectful classroom for all students.

BRAVO (Building Relationships with Actions that Value Others) teachers must be committed to actions that establish respect for *all* students, parents, and faculty throughout the school. Respectful schools are a result of respectful classrooms, and respectful classrooms are led by respectful teachers. Respectful teachers establish a classroom climate where *all* students are able to ask questions and contribute their own ideas. However, in a recent study, researchers observed more than 350 math and science lessons and found that only 45% received high ratings for respect (Weiss & Pasley, 2004). Respect is a very basic concept that treats everyone with dignity. Actions that are respectful demonstrate that all people are important, their ideas are worthwhile, and the jobs they do are valuable contributions to the school. Simply put, treating others with respect means treating *all* people the way you would like to be treated. The individual is important, every individual. Teacher actions that emphasize respect for *all* are fair and caring.

Respect for All by Being Fair

There was a time in our schools where we thought that respect for students could be ensured with the concept of *equality*; today we are more concerned with *equity*. What is the difference? According to Edmund Gordon, "Equality requires sameness, but equity requires that treatments be appropriate and sufficient to [meet] ...needs" (Pang, 2005, p. 263). In the classroom equitable treatment is generally translated as fairness. "That's not fair!" As teachers, we hear this many times daily, whether we teach kindergarten, high school, or university classes—somehow, somewhere, sometime, someway, something, or someone just won't be fair!

Fairness is one of the most challenging, misinterpreted concepts in the classroom. Most people who are concerned about fairness confuse equity with equality. They think that everyone should be treated equally—exactly the same in all circumstances. But there is a time to treat students equally and a time to treat students equitably. Think about it, is it right to treat every child *exactly* the same in *every* circumstance? BRAVO teachers implement fairness by understanding the difference between equality and equity. They know when to emphasize equality by treating students the same without bias or favoritism and when to be equitable and treat students differently to meet different needs. They also understand they must be consistent.

Treat Students Equally Without Bias

Teachers should be fair, and we should not have favorite students in our classes—just say NO to teacher's pets! But the truth is that some students, parents, and co-workers are just easier to like than others. So, let's be truthful—of course, teachers have favorites. When we acknowledge that we have favorites at school, then, and only then, can we make a conscious decision to treat all students in our classrooms without bias and free of favoritism. Stop reading for a moment and ask yourself these questions:

+ Do I have more patience with some students, than with others?

+ Do I call on the same students every day?

+ Do I ask the same students for help when I need an errand run?

+ Do I engage the same students in conversation, and rarely talk with others?

+ Do I grade assignments differently for different students?

+ Do I help some students more willingly than others?

+ Do I expect some students to achieve high academic standards while expecting little from others?

If you did not answer yes to even one of the questions, I commend you on your fairness! Go to the head of the class! But, if you are like me, and you answered yes to at least one of the questions, you are guilty of not being fair and of favoritism or bias. Although this is not *true confessions,* being honest with yourself and identifying that sometimes you react unfairly is the first step toward having a classroom that is fair. We cannot change until we recognize the need for change. Now move to step 2 and reflect on when and why this happens. Then, of course, move to step 3, which is to consciously change unfair actions and treat *all* children without bias or favoritism.

Lana was in my fifth-grade class. She was quiet, rarely got in trouble, completed all class assignments nicely, did her homework, and got along well with the other students. One evening, I received a telephone call from her mother who told me: "Lana has been crying since she got home from school today; she says that you do not like her at all." I was shocked. Of course, I liked Lana. Then, the mother went on to list all the things that I was doing, or not doing, that indicated that I did not like her daughter, such as never calling on her and never asking her to do anything special for me.

After I hung up the phone, I was angry—at Lana. How dare she think that I didn't like her! Then, I began to make excuses for myself. Of course, I liked Lana, but I had a large class, and there just wasn't time to do *everything.* After I finished making excuses for myself, I began to make excuses for Lana. After all, she was quiet and did everything so well, she just did not need as much attention as other students. Then, I began to play the day over in my mind, and the day before, and the day before that. In my memory, I tried to recall what I had done to involve Lana, had I called on her as often as others? Was I treating her differently? Yes, I was. Why was I doing this? It was not that I did not like Lana; she was just so quiet and so unobtrusive that it was easy to focus on other students. Lana needed me to demonstrate openly that I liked her. Over the next few days, I made sure that I spoke to her when she came into the room and called on her in class. My anger and excuses melted away; and in its place was a new resolve to *consciously* treat *all* of my students with respect and to treat them equally without bias or favoritism.

Then, of course, there is the school board president's son or daughter and the challenge of treating this student so that others don't accuse you of favoritism. It isn't easy, but you must. Can you hug the child who hasn't bathed? You should, he needs that hug more than anyone.

One morning when I was on hall duty, I was casually visiting with middle school students waiting for school to begin. They began talking about one of their teachers. One of the boys said, "Miss Smith is really fair!" I asked why he thought that. "Because she likes all of us just the same." BRAVO teachers acknowledge their weaknesses, reflect on their actions, and moment by moment, they act with fairness to treat students equally regardless of who their parents are, their ethnicity, their socioeconomic status, or other arbitrary considerations. They consciously choose to *never* treat children differently out of bias or favoritism.

Meet Different Needs Equitably

Another aspect of fairness that creates a problem for some teachers is how to equitably meet the needs of different students with different abilities, temperaments, and life circumstances and still be considered fair to all students. This is what makes the concept of fairness so complex, because there are times when it is not only appropriate to treat students differently, it is mandated, or simply in their best interests. Although teachers who are fair treat students equally without bias, they also know when to treat students differently (equitably) to meet their different needs.

Treating students differently is necessary when students identified through special education have an Individual Education Plan (IEP) that identifies a need for modifications in curriculum, instruction, or assessment which must be followed. In other words, based on their particular need, these students are given extended testing time, are allowed to be tested orally, have assignments reduced, and participate in other revisions. I know teachers who feel this is not fair; after all, other students in their class are not receiving the same instruction. To these teachers I remind them that this is mandated by the law and if the modifications are not implemented they are breaking the law. Despite their personal feelings, this kind of different treatment is fair and based on a need to be equitable.

Then there are life circumstances, a death or illness in the family, a parent out of a job, a new baby in the family, limited understanding of the language, or other stressful situations where instruction and assignments should be modified. Unlike mandated modifications where the decision is made for us, these depend on our understanding of the concept of fairness, which I call the "know when to hold'em and when to fold'em" concept. When I was a principal, I remember a first-year teacher who met with me after a student in her class had complained that she was not being fair. It seems that a struggling student in her junior English class had failed to turn in his final paper on time which meant that he would fail the class. Knowing that the boy, the sole support of his mother who was very ill, held two different late-night jobs, she allowed him to submit his paper on the next day. The teacher came to me questioning if she had done the right thing. I gave her the same answer that I have always given to students, parents, and other teachers who might have that concern:

> Sometimes we have different needs, if you (or your child) had a need that required a revised assignment I would do the same for you. Fair does not mean treating all students in exactly the same way. *Fair means treating students in the way they should be treated to meet their needs.* If I hurt my leg and needed a crutch to walk, would you deny me that help unless everyone walked with a crutch? I don't think so. Fair does not mean equal, it means equitable.

I'm reminded of the fourth grader who was required to write all of 50 states and their capitals. He studied hard for the test and recited all of the states and capitals perfectly for me at recess when I was on duty. The next day, I saw him and asked how he did. He looked crestfallen and said that he had failed the test. I was amazed. When I saw his teacher later that day, I commented how surprised I was because he had recited them so effortlessly at recess. "Oh," she said, "he knew them just fine, but he spelled most of them wrong." Without thinking, I asked, "Was this a spelling assignment or a social studies assignment?" It was a social studies assignment. As I walked away, I couldn't help but consider how unfair this was. The grade in the social studies column indicated that he did not know the states and capitals. But, in truth, he did. He just did not know how to spell them.

Our students are not all the same. They learn at different rates; as author Michael Carr wrote, "All children are gifted; some just open their packages earlier than others" (Blaydes, 2003, p. 46). They learn in different ways, so if students can't learn the way we teach, we must teach the way they learn. If one student needs more help than another, we must be prepared to provide that help. Teachers must be sensitive to the different life circumstances of students. When there is a need, being fair means that we *should* be equitable and treat students differently if we are going to do what we are called to do as teachers—facilitate student learning. Certainly being a teacher is about teaching, but more than that, being a teacher is about learning! This concept of fairness in the classroom builds respectful relationships when it is extended to all of our students.

Emphasize Consistency

Teachers who are described as fair and respected by students and parents are also consistent. It is when teachers are consistent that students learn to trust that their teacher will make every effort to be fair. How can teachers be consistent when I have just emphasized that BRAVO teachers meet different student needs in different ways, which sounds inconsistent? Being consistent means that our actions are predictable enough that students can *with confidence* count on us to respond in a certain way most of the time. Obviously, this suggests that consistency can be a bad thing if we always make poor decisions. But when students understand that we will always try to make decisions that meet their individual student needs, they can trust us to be appropriately consistent. When students understand that we will treat all students equally without bias or favoritism and not be arbitrary and react one way for one student and then respond one way for another student just because—students are able to trust our consistency.

Teachers establish a climate of respect in the classroom by being fair. I overheard two high school students in the hall arguing about how fair one of their teacher's was. One of the students said, "He's not fair at all because he doesn't always treat us the same. When I was late to class last week, I got in trouble. When you were late to class, he didn't say anything. That's not fair!" The other student responded, "But you are always late to class, when I was late last week, I had been at my grandmother's funeral. That's why he's fair. You can always count on him to treat us like individuals." When teachers treat students and others fairly, we demonstrate that people are more important than isolated rules. While it is necessary to have rules, our classroom rules should have some "wiggle room" to allow us to make decisions that meet student needs fairly and wisely.

Teachers demonstrate fairness by treating all students equally without bias, by treating students equitably to meet special student needs, and by being consistent in doing this. In other words, teachers must know when to hold'em and when to fold'em. When students trust us to be fair, we build relationships of respect.

Respecting Others
with Actions That Are Caring

Nel Noddings (1992) argues that our aim as educators should be to educate children who are "competent, caring, loving, and lovable people" (p. xiv). Most teachers would agree with this because we care about students that we teach. We don't teach math, reading, history—we teach students, and BRAVO teachers are constantly mindful of this. Caring is about making connections with students; we teach students, not books! I cringe when I hear teachers say, "I teach math." No! We do not teach math, we teach math to students!

Caring about students is far more than just warm and fuzzy sentiment, in fact, according to Sergiovanni (1992) the ethic of care is the key to academic success! Yet, in an unpublished study I did a few years ago with 60 high school students in an urban area and 60 high school students in a rural area, using random selection, only 32% of the students said that they had a teacher who cared about them! Noddings (1992) reports a Girl Scout study where only one third of the students in the survey felt that their teachers cared for them and only 7% said they would go to a teacher for advice. This same survey found that one child in 100 claimed that *no adult* cared for him or her!

I am dismayed that as many as two out of every three of our students feel that teachers do not care about them. I hope the truth is that teachers who don't care for students are in a very small minority; sadly, it is probably also true that some teachers care for only some of their students. But BRAVO teachers care deeply about *all* of their students. In fact, we should love our students—all of them. We can't let our students think we don't care about them or that we don't love them, so we must work smarter at implementing actions that leave no doubt how much we care for our students. I have heard it said that "students don't care what you know until they know that you care." I believe this is true, but even more "no one cares what you say, if your actions don't say that you care" (Harris, 2004, p. 38). If students don't think we care, we need to change our behaviors so that they will know that we care. Teachers who respect students make the most of teaching moments to demonstrate their care for each individual student by being sensitive, by nurturing growth, and by seeking balance. These actions build relationships that value students.

Be Sensitive

An article in the *USA Today* recently caught my eye. It was titled "A Community of Kindness" and featured a U.S. Department of Defense teacher in Germany, Pamela Hall (McEntee, 2004, p. 6D). The article described the many things she does to create a caring, "loving environment," so that school is a "secure place in an insecure world." Hall's principal noted that it was "her enthusiasm, energy, skill, and sense of what each child needs [that enabled her to] reach each child, regardless of who the student is." Teachers who are sensitive to all students engage them in conversation, listen to their concerns, and watch them in class, in the halls, on the playground, and getting off the bus. Being sensitive to students is not acting in "warm, fuzzy" ways. In fact, being sensitive is more than just being aware it is a *heightened awareness and understanding of students and their individual needs.*

One evening, just before the university semester ended last year, my students in a principalship class were presenting class projects. One student, teaching in an especially poor neighborhood, shared about a tutorial program to meet the academic needs of students of poverty. While working after school with the children she became aware that some of her students did not look forward to the weekends. With tears running down her face, she pointed out that many of these children would not have a hot meal, or enough to eat until they came back to school on the following Monday. Being sensitive to this led her to send children home with healthy snacks in their backpacks every Friday.

There was a boy in my sixth grade class one year who was one of those very self-sufficient students who really didn't seem to need a teacher. With just a little guidance he could pick up any concept, he was popular with his classmates—boys and girls alike considered him a favorite. His sense of humor often kept the whole class laughing, and, he was a good athlete. He was a pleasure in the classroom. One day, after school was out and children were waiting for the bus, he sat down on the curb and buried his face in his hands. As I stood by, I watched his shoulders shake and, suddenly, I heard great sobs. I walked over to him, put my arm around his shoulders and asked what was wrong. In one miserable, hurried sentence, he cried, "My Dad has left my Mom, we have to move, and no one can help me." My heart broke for him, and I gave him the only thing I could at that moment, a hug. Being sensitive to our students reminds us that there is so much more to teaching school when we look beyond the pencil and paper and glimpse into the heart and hurt of a child.

Sensitive teachers notice when changes take place in children's lives and try to do something about it. Noticing that there are children who don't come to school when the weather turns cold may lead to a free "Clothing Closet." Being sensitive that a student cannot see the board clearly may be as simple as a classroom seating change, or it may need a referral to the school nurse. Noticing that a child whose parents are going through a divorce is unusually quiet, lethargic, and sad over a period of time may result in a referral to Social Services for counseling support.

In a recent study on peer harassment, a colleague and I found that 77% of students reported that bullying happened at least "sometimes" in the classroom (Harris & Petrie, 2002; Harris, Petrie & Willoughby, 2002). Sensitive teachers notice the dynamics of student relationships within the class setting. When children are teased or called names, they do not permit this kind of behavior. They note when children are alone, not included, or teased and do what they can to help that child belong and find a friend.

Sensitive teachers notice when boyfriends and girlfriends break up and offer advice or a consoling hug. They notice when a student's grades drop and they investigate to understand what is happening in that child's life. Recently a picture came over the Internet; I don't know if the story that came with it is true or not. It was a picture of twin babies. One baby was weak and possibly not going to live—the other was healthy. Going against hospital rules, the nurse put the babies together in the same incubator. The healthy sister placed her arm over the sick baby. Before long the unhealthy twin's heart rate stabilized, and the baby grew to become healthy. I hope this story is true; but even if not, it is a poignant reminder to teachers of the power of the moment, being sensitive to our students' needs, and reaching out with a caring touch.

Someone once said that people will forget what you said but never how you made them feel. Sensitive teachers respect students and care as much about how they make students feel as they care about teaching academics. Stop for a moment and reflect on your teachers when you were in school. What do you remember most—the facts you were taught, or how they made you feel? By being sensitive to students' needs, teachers build relationships that value students.

Nurture Growth

Caring actions go beyond being sensitive, kind, and compassionate. Teachers who truly care deeply about students implement actions that motivate and nurture growth in their students even when students appear to resist that help. They push and pull to nurture growth that holds all children to a high standard.

I heard a story about a teacher who received a parrot as a gift just before Thanksgiving. The parrot had a lousy attitude and every word out of the bird's mouth was rude, obnoxious, and profane. The teacher tried to change the bird's attitude by role modeling only polite words, and treating him with kindness. But none of this worked. Frustrated, the teacher yelled at the parrot and the parrot yelled back. He shook the parrot and the parrot got even angrier and more rude. Finally, in desperation, he grabbed the parrot and put him in the freezer. The parrot squawked and screamed. But suddenly, it got very quiet and not a peep was heard from the parrot. Fearing that the parrot was hurt, the teacher opened the freezer.

The parrot calmly stepped out onto his owner's outstretched arms and said, "I believe I may have offended you with my rude language and actions. I am sincerely remorseful for my inappropriate transgressions and I fully intend to do everything I can to correct my rude behavior."

The teacher was stunned at the change in the bird's attitude. As he was about to ask the parrot what had made such a dramatic change in his behavior, the bird continued courteously, "May I ask what the turkey did?" (Remember, this was around Thanksgiving!)

I know you are thinking what does a profane parrot have to do with caring actions that nurture growth? Sometimes, students, like the profane parrot, do not listen to our suggestions. Realizing that putting them in a freezer is not an option, still we must find ways to challenge and nurture their growth. We can never give up on our students.

In the same study I mentioned earlier where so many students reported that many of their teachers did not care about them, I asked them what teachers did to demonstrate that they cared for them. More than half of the students focused on actions where teachers challenged them to do better work or be better people. Here are just a few of the phrases that were used most often: "helps you to pass," "makes us do our work," "makes learning fun," "worries when I'm not doing well," "pushes me to do more than I think I can," "calls my parents when I don't do my work," "helps me with advice about my boyfriend," "works with me to not get in trouble," "doesn't let me get away with being lazy," and "reminds me that I can do this."

One of my aspiring principal students designed a math tutorial and required that students attend if their grades dropped. He shared this note from one of the sophomores who had to participate:

> For years all I can remember is that I hated math. I even dreaded it, but ever since Mr. M. started this new and fun way of teaching the class math, even though I have to come after school, I have actually enjoyed math and can't wait to come here! And also I am finally passing math for the first time in years. Since last year, my grade in this class has improved 30 to 35 points. I back him up 100% in doing this class. Mr. M. really cares for us.

BRAVO teachers do not give zeroes. They do not let students fall through the cracks. Because they respect and care for students, they stand firm in their resolve to push for growth, sometimes with a gentle nudge, and sometimes with greater insistence.

Nurturing growth in students means that teachers must find ways to motivate them. One way to do this is to follow William Glasser's Choice Theory (1998). Choice theory nurtures growth by meeting student needs in five areas (an example is given for each):

♦ Survival—Adopt classroom rules that emphasize treating others with respect.

- Love and Belonging—Involve students in team-building activities.
- Power—Implement a variety of instructional strategies.
- Freedom—Give opportunities for students to have input in the class.
- Fun—Develop games for review sessions.

Teachers who respect their students, understand the importance of actions that are caring yet challenging to nurture growth.

Seek Balance

All around us the world reverberates in the need for balance in our lives. Too much sun scorches the earth, too much shade prevents the grass from growing, too much rain causes rivers to rise from their banks, and too much food makes us fat, yet all of these things are necessary for life. Too much duty makes us dull, but too much fun makes us flighty. Too much discipline is dangerous, but too much mercy creates mayhem.

As teachers, we are constantly seeking balance in how we work with students because we are stretched in so many directions. We must emphasize academics so that every student will achieve, and we must also build relationships so that students can get along in a complex, changing world. If we are not careful and things get out of balance, we become rigid and unmerciful in our demands for students to learn, or we become so emotional with the sad situations in which some of our children live due to poverty or other family situations that we demand nothing. We become so concerned with discipline that we allow no freedom in our classrooms at all. Then again, we become so concerned with freedom that we leave out responsibility, and our classrooms are chaotic. I have seen it both ways; but it is caring that helps us find a balance.

I once taught next door to a teacher who had just graduated with a teaching degree from a very prestigious university. She had wonderful lesson plans, detailed, masterful, and highly creative. Unfortunately, she had absolutely no discipline in her class, so her marvelous lesson plans were absolutely useless. She constantly blamed the students for their misbehavior. "Why did I get the bad class?" she would moan at lunch. Our team taught third grade at that school, and when the other teachers went into her room to teach their lessons, the children worked very well. The problem was not with the students, it was with the teacher. She had forgotten to balance good lesson plans with a balanced approach to discipline and a classroom management plan.

Achieving balance is most likely to happen when teachers spend time in self-reflection. In reflecting on our actions, if we put everything on a continuum, most of the time we try to end up somewhere in the middle. On the one hand, if the classroom is silent and students are sitting the better part of the day just listening (or day dreaming, more likely), then there is a lack of balance. On the other hand, if the classroom is so noisy and busy with movement that the teacher can't be heard and students can't work, then there is a lack of balance. Students should have an opportunity to talk, and they should have the opportunity to move about the room, but the teacher should be able to be heard and students should be able to work without distractions.

One way to be reminded of the need for balance is to invite peers to observe the classroom with a stop watch. How much of the time do they observe children who are engaged, dynamic, and animated? How much of the time do they observe children who are bored or disengaged? I observed in a classroom one time where the teacher was leading a reading lesson to a small group of second graders. The students sat in their circle of chairs with books on their laps, and they each read a paragraph. The teacher's lesson plan indicated that the object of the lesson was vocabulary building. But there they sat, reading one by one, in monotone voices—students lost their place and daydreamed until it was their turn to read, while the teacher yawned and frowned because the children were not paying close attention. Instead, she could have played a simple game with them ("Put your finger on the word I am talking about: I see a word on this page that rhymes with play"), or had the students pantomime the words, or any number of other simple, fun ideas that reinforce vocabulary.

You can gauge your own balance without a person or a stop-watch, just count the yawns—too many, too often, are an indication that something is out of balance. Remember, if you are bored, imagine how the children feel. Strive for balance with facts and fun, and in learning and laughter, when planning the school day.

Humor is a wonderful way to show respect for students in a caring, balanced way that builds relationships. Laughter also makes us feel better and can increase circulation and even block pain (Gorrow, 2004). After all, "He who laughs, lasts" (Mary Pettibone Poole, Bullivant, 2004, p. 87). Laughter creates strong connections. One year when I was teaching elementary students, we needed a piano player. Not one of the staff could play the piano but me, and I could only barely play. But I volunteered to help anyway. Every Thursday, I would stumble through the music session while the boys and girls bravely tried to cover up the wrong notes I played. Then, one day we had a guest speaker who sat down at the piano, announced he had never had a piano lesson in his life, and proceeded to tell a story accompanied by marvelous music for 30 minutes. The children were enchanted. When my students and I got back to the classroom, one of the boys looked at me and announced to the whole class, "Boy, I bet you were jealous." I still smile when I remember how we all enjoyed a good laugh—at my expense.

Teachers should never use sarcasm, even with older students, for fear of hurting their feelings or being misunderstood. However, humor often helps us achieve that much-needed balance; but sometimes our laughter must be silent. I still laugh (to myself) when I remember the Thanksgiving essay one of my third-grade students wrote about the *penguins* who came over on the Mayflower. I laugh (silently) when I think of the first grader who introduced me to her mother as "the queen of the school," (I was the principal). And I still smile when I remember the first grader who walked up to me, tugged on my sleeve and said, "You can't be the president . . . you're a girl." (principal, president—get it?)

BRAVO teachers laugh often with their students —but usually at themselves. One teacher noted that her students love it when she makes a mistake at the board. "When they find an error, I always say, in mock horror, 'Not me! Why, I never make mistakes.' My class loves this." Some teachers say, "Oh, I did that just to see if you were paying attention," which usually gets a laugh. Other teachers bring in cartoons and share these with the class. Laughing with our students builds positive relationships.

Even with the challenging requirements of the No Child Left Behind Act (NCLB), there are still ways to balance academic lessons by incorporating games as an occasional instructional delivery method. But even here there must be a balance and the learning should balance with the fun. In my first year of teaching, one day I thought it would be a great idea to play History Baseball or something like that. In no time, what started as a fun way to review for an up-coming test deteriorated into a loud, noisy, unruly group of 10 year olds and the teacher (me) had to stop the game. The next time we did this, we created a set of game rules for the classroom first!

Establishing a climate of respect at school means that caring teachers must be sensitive, nurture growth, and seek a balance in all they do. Through these actions we build valuing relationships with individual students.

Tactical Actions That Respect Others

What tactical actions can BRAVO teachers implement that build relationships that value others through respect?

+ Treat students as individuals.
+ Become better acquainted with students and their families.
+ Evaluate when students are treated differently.
+ Evaluate why students are treated differently.
+ Treat people the way you like to be treated.
+ Treat students the way you would like your children to be treated.

- Talk with students about their lives in and out of class.
- Use duty times to interact with students.
- Share parts of your life with students.
- Be observant of classroom interactions.
- Be available to talk with students about their concerns in and out of school.
- Collaborate with students to develop classroom rules.
- Challenge students to think and to ask questions.
- Share your concern for students when they are not doing well academically.
- Expect students to do their best.
- Contact parents when there is a need.
- Provide tutorial assistance.
- Evaluate class activities and instructional delivery for balance.
- Balance learning and laughter; facts and fun.
- Observe other teachers.
- Video your classroom.
- Laugh with your students.

Teachers who teach with their heart respect students, other faculty and parents, and build communities of learning undergirded by strong relationships. It is in respectful classrooms where students are valued as individuals that they learn to make connections to the world they live in and beyond. Children, like Jason, who have difficulty finding a place to belong continue to remind us to make the most of our moments to teach "with respect" for all of our students.

Remember, BRAVO teachers build relationships with actions that value others by demonstrating respect for all.

> *Actions That Demonstrate Respect for All*
> **Every Individual Is Important**
>
> **Respect All by Being Fair**
> - Treat Students Equally Without Bias
> - Meet Different Needs Equitably
> - Emphasize Consistency
>
> **Respect Others with Actions That Are Caring**
> - Be Sensitive
> - Nurture Growth
> - Seek Balance

4

Actions
That Support All
Students—Rekindle
the Inner Spirit

We should all be thankful for those people who rekindle the inner spirit.

Albert Schweitzer

Keith was in the third grade, although he was already 10. He was tall, at least a head taller than the other boys in the class. He had blonde hair and blue eyes and freckles across the bridge of his nose. He was the biggest boy in our class, and very athletic, but also the gentlest with a ready smile. On the playground, when other children started arguing, he somehow brought about peaceful resolution. In the classroom, when other children got rowdy, he continued to work hard. Kirk's oral vocabulary was years ahead of most other classmates. He particularly loved science and knew just about everything there was to know about animals.

Every day Keith and I sat in the back of the room—a reading group of two. He was in the third grade for the second time. We would open the reader, and he would sound out the letters on the page. He would bend his head down close to the page, as if he were closer to the words they would become clearer to him. His brow furrowed as he tried to read each word. But Keith could not read. I tried different approaches to help him—phonics, whole word, trade books—but he could not read. I worked with his parents, counseled with other teachers, and sought help at the local university, but he made little progress. Still, every day he came expectantly to the reading table, a smile on his face, his book in hand, ready to try again, and every day it was my job to be sure to greet him with a smile of support.

The year was 1972, and I did not teach Keith to read that year. Over the years, I have not forgotten him; instead, he continues to remind me of the importance of the wide-ranging support that teachers are called upon to give. I was there to support Keith in his learning, in his attempts to learn, and in dealing with failure when learning didn't happen. In other words, I was there to rekindle his spirit from day to day so that he would not give up.

There is an old saying that the difference between heaven and hell is that in hell there is not enough food to feed yourself, but in heaven there is enough food to feed even your neighbor. BRAVO (Building Relationships with Actions that Value Others) teachers always have support to offer to their students, and the well of support never runs dry. Supportive teachers who build relationships with actions that value others make the most of every moment to communicate effectively and offer encouragement.

Support Actions Communicate Effectively

Supportive communication is vital to rekindling the spirit. In fact, the National Parent Teacher Association (NPTA, 1997) lists regular, meaningful communication between home and school as the first of six standards to be met in supporting students. Yet, our actions often communicate more than we realize. A teacher may say verbally that he is there to help students whenever they need assistance. However, if students come to his desk, and he continues grading a paper, or if his voice has an unpleasant edge, or if he is rarely available to meet with parents, it doesn't matter what he said. His actions have communicated just the opposite: He is too busy to help students. This is especially serious, because according to Dr. Joyce Brothers, after one negative communication or encounter, it takes seven to eight positive encounters to change an opinion. Typically, only 20% of students feel that they have an adult at school that they can talk to. Even worse, on average, parents spend 12.5 minutes a day talking with their children, and 8.5 minutes are discouraging conversation. Communication is necessary for support, but for it to be effective, we must be truthful, listen actively, and be available.

Be Truthful

Truthful communication is not easy because it frequently means that we must tell people what they do not want to hear. I am reminded of the first grader one day who was at my desk asking a question, when he looked at me and said, "You have really old hands." (I was 24 at the time!) Truth telling, not done with sensitivity, can destroy a relationship that took years to build or stop a relationship before it even begins. Unlike George Washington, who could not tell a lie, most of us are not so single-minded. Yet as teachers, we find ourselves in circumstances where if we do not tell the truth, we cannot support students properly with the help they need. It takes courage to tell the truth, but it also takes trust and tact.

The purpose of telling the truth in the context of communicating effectively as teachers is to help students. With this in mind, we must make sure that speaking truthfully achieves the desired result. When we have a trusting, positive relationship with a student or with parents, it is much easier not only to speak the truth but for that truth to be received properly. This is why it is critical that our actions demonstrate to parents and students that our purpose is always to better serve students.

Communicating effectively requires a complex skill, called tact, which Howard Newton defined as the "art of making a point without making an enemy" (Blaydes, 2003, p. 63), and Orlando Battista defined as the "ability to make a person see the lightning without letting him feel the bolt" (Blaydes, 2003, p. 69). The very definition of tact emphasizes how important it is to communicate truth calmly, using words that do not convey negative emotions whenever possible. For example, we may feel that a student who never finishes class assignments is just being lazy. To bluntly tell parents their child is lazy, you might as well tell them that you think they are lazy. In addition to probably making an enemy, other possible reactions to this effort at truth telling include:

- Parents reacting protectively —"Oh, he's just so creative, his mind is on other things."
- Parents taking the comment personally — "Well, he's just like me!"
- Parents perceiving the comment as an indictment on their parenting skills — "Well, I've tried to change him."
- Parents and student placing blame — "She never really liked our child (me) in the first place."

When teachers find a way to speak the truth tactfully, it is much more likely to be received and at the same time result in building strong, supportive relationships with the student and the parent. Early in my teaching career, I learned an approach to addressing concerns truthfully that my principal called the "sandwich method." This was placing concern comments between more positive statements whenever it was possible. Sure enough, I found that parents were usually more likely to cooperate when I would say, "Johnny has a wonderful sense of humor. However, it is often difficult to motivate him to complete assignments in class. By the way, I am enjoying having Johnny in my class this year. I wonder if you have some suggestions that might help me help Johnny finish his work?" Almost without fail, the parent response would be something like this: "Yes, I find that he can be *lazy* at home, too. How can I help?" They can say "lazy," but we can't! When you use the sandwich method, be sure to make your point clearly and don't sugarcoat it so much that parents or students fail to hear the true issue.

As teachers, if we expect to be truthful with our students, we should give them opportunities to give us truthful input. BRAVO teachers, whether teaching first grade or university students, always have students evaluate their teaching. We ask them to tell us what they have liked, what they have not liked, and to make suggestions so we can improve the class. Then, we remind them to tell us the truth, but be tactful.

Listen Actively

Teachers who are good listeners have mastered an important skill for supporting students and building relationships in the classroom. In fact, there is a saying that the reason God gave us two ears and one mouth was so we would listen twice as much as we talk! To build strong support relationships with our students, busy teachers rarely *find* time to listen, so we must *make time to listen.* There is no quicker way to cause others to feel of little value than to say, while continuing to work, "Go ahead, I'm listening." You might as well say "You are not important enough for me to listen to," because that is what is being communicated. Listening supports students, parents, and other faculty, while it also communicates respect for them.

One of the few memories I have of my own elementary school experience happened when I was in the fifth grade. My new baby sister had just been born, and I was very excited—so excited that I went to school early. My teacher was on the playground visiting with another teacher. I went up to her and stood quietly at first. Then, I tried desperately to make eye contact. Finally, I called out, "Guess what?" My teacher looked at me and said very sternly, "Can't you see I'm busy?" I turned away from her, bitterly disappointed that I could not share my news. All day long I expected her to ask about my news—but she never did.

As teachers, we must do more than listen; we must listen *actively* to support our students. This communicates that we care, that we value what they have to tell us, and, ultimately, that they are important to us. One year I asked my third graders to evaluate our class, and I was reminded of the importance of active listening. The students turned in their evaluations, and when school was over that day, I eagerly sat down to read them. It was a great class; I was thoroughly enjoying the year; and the notes confirmed that the students were having a good year, too. Then I picked up the last folded piece of notebook paper. It said very simply:

You don't care if we lose things.

Amanda.

What did she mean? I wasn't aware of any problems with Amanda at all. The next day when she came to school, I asked her in my most pleasant voice if there was something that she had lost at school. (Following up must be handled very carefully, because if students are going to speak freely, they can't feel intimidated. We can't rekindle the spirit if we break the spirit!). Immediately, Amanda described an incident that happened the previous week. She couldn't find a book and thought that it was still outside on the playground. When she told me about this that day, I nodded and said, "Oh, you'll find it." Then I went on with whatever we were doing and didn't think of it again. But Amanda did not forget.

Active listening means we hear and then do something about what we hear. It implies action that responds to what is being said. Listening without responding is almost as bad as not listening in the first place. Another way that teachers demonstrate active listening is to repeat what we have heard: "So you're telling me that ..." This also helps clarify what was said and is a good way to prevent misunderstandings. Active listening communicates to our students that we are here to support them. Playground duty, hall duty, and bus duty can be transformed from unpleasant chores to valuable times for informal dialogue with students. Talking with students provides a valuable support and introduces us to a dimension of the student that we might not otherwise know. We become aware of talents and interests, and are provided with insights into problems a student may be having at school or at home.

Be Available

BRAVO teachers provide parents at the beginning of the year with ways that they can communicate and be available. Most teachers give times when parents can call them at home, or provide them with an e-mail address. Most of our schools today have websites, which makes communication even easier, and parents are encouraged to go to the website where lesson plans and other classroom information are provided for them.

Scheduling time to meet with parents and students face to face is critical. Over the years, I have generally found it much more preferable to talk in person, especially with unhappy or concerned parents to have a more open, candid dialogue. There is power in reaching to touch a parent's hand and just saying, "I'm sorry, how can I help," that builds relationships and has defused many crises. It's too easy when talking on the phone to come across the wrong way, which can be devastating to teacher/student/parent relationships. Often, handwritten notes or e-mail can be misunderstood or mistakes made, like the note this second-grade teacher sent home: "Please talk with John about his behavior. He is disruptive and acting just like a child." (This is a real note, honest. What did the teacher expect? Always, always have someone proofread any note that you send home!) Parents can make mistakes on notes, also, like this one: "Tommy is under a doctor's care and should not take P.E. today. Please execute him."

Another way that teachers support students and their families is to make home visits. I will never forget a home visit that I made in my third year of teaching. Gay was a chubby, little third grader with a quiet smile. Her complexion was ruddy, and her cheeks were always red, as though she wore too much rouge. Her clothes were soiled hand-me-downs, and her hair was rarely brushed. She was a good student, and her attendance was excellent. But Gay did not make friends easily, and she often annoyed her classmates because she was always borrowing paper, pencils, or crayons from them. When we had parent night at the beginning of the year, her parents did not come. On the first day of school, she came with an older sister. I decided it was time to meet her parents, so I made a home visit.

I drove down a country dirt road to Gay's home—an old two-story, used-to-be-white house that sat at the end of a small lane. I walked by mounds of trash that were piled in the yard, and somewhat shakily avoided two big dogs that were barking and running up to greet me. I stepped onto the porch and knocked on the screen door. Eight-year-old Gay opened the door holding a baby in her arms, while a toddler held on to her dress. She smiled that quiet smile that I often saw in class and called to her mother, who was in the kitchen. Gay's mother handed supper duties over to an older sibling, and we visited for a few minutes. It was a pleasant talk, and I bragged on Gay's attendance and her academic potential. After this brief contact, Gay's mother came to the Christmas program that December and to the parent night in the spring. This one visit to Gay's home gave me a deeper understanding of Gay. I made sure that she never had to borrow paper, pencils, or crayons from classmates again that year.

When teachers build relationships with students and their families, they implement actions that communicate their support of students by being truthful, listening actively, and being available. The more we know about our students, their parents, and other faculty members, the more support we can provide.

Support Actions to Encourage

There is an African story that goes like this: An old man is dying, and he calls his people to his side. He gives a short,

sturdy stick to each of his many offspring, wives, and rela-
tives. "Break the stick," he instructs them. With some effort,
they all snap their sticks in half. "This is how it is when a soul
is alone without anyone. They can be easily broken." The old
man next gives each of his kin another stick, and says, "This is
how I would like for you to live after I pass. Put your sticks together in bundles of twos and threes. Now, break these bundles in half." No one can break the sticks when there are two
or more in a bundle, and the old man smiles. We are strong
when we stand with another soul (Estes, 1992).

When teachers stand with another soul, they encourage
others with hope, courage, and confidence to rekindle the
spirit. This kind of encouraging support is demonstrated by
actions that build confidence, actions that are positive, actions
that are persistent, and actions that provide resources.

Build Confidence

One way that teachers build confidence in students is to
build their self-esteem. When we demonstrate our belief that
students can do something and then support them in doing it,
they begin to believe in themselves. These kinds of supportive
relationships build people up rather than tear them down.
When students believe in themselves, it's amazing what can
be accomplished. The great athlete Althea Gibson attributed
half her success to "[being] game enough to take a lot of pun-
ishment along the way and half because there were a lot of
people who cared enough to help me" (Eisen, 1995).

In addition to telling students when they do well privately, teachers build confidence in students when we recognize their talents publicly. I taught a graduate class recently on
the campus of an alternative high school. One night I arrived
at my class early. Except for an administrator and a few teachers grading papers, the building seemed deserted. I noticed
that the hallway was lined with poems written by the students. As I began slowly walking down the hall reading the
poems, a young man came up to me and asked if I needed directions. I told him that I was waiting for my class to start, but
that I was enjoying reading the poems. He said, "They really

are good, aren't they?" Then, with just a hint of pride, he asked, "Would you like to read mine?"

In one of my doctoral classes recently, all the students submitted a chapter they were writing for a project, except one student. He quit answering my e-mails and would not accept my phone calls. I kept calling. When I finally reached him, I said, "I'll be at your office tomorrow at two." We met, and I read his paper. I noted that it started really well, then I added transitional words here and there, made a few suggestions and said that I really liked his paper (here's that sandwich again!). I pointed out where it was strong and how we had already fixed some of the weak places with just those few suggestions. When he left, he turned to me and said, "I knew I could do this."

Building confidence in our students is not telling them they can do something that we know they cannot do. The impossible dream is impossible unless we begin with the possible; there is no building without a foundation! Confidence grows every time a student accomplishes the possible. By knowing our students, we identify their foundational learning, and that is where we begin. Then we instill confidence by supporting students to take the first step, succeed; take the second step, succeed; and eventually they can continue on their own journey. Often teachers have to go back several skill levels to find that possible skill. Once students begin to believe in themselves with confidence, they are inspired to do more. Confident students, when they meet failure (as most of us are sure to do), have the strength to see failure in the right perspective—as part of the journey—not the destination. Remember, Babe Ruth struck out 1,330 times on his way to hitting 714 home runs (and this was before steroids).

Use Positive Action

To encourage students we must be positive and focus on what they can do, not what they cannot do. Yet, the average elementary student receives three negative comments for every positive one. Middle school students hear nine negative comments for every positive one, and high school students hear 11 to 17 negative comments for every positive comment they hear! We must find ways to be positive and constructive to help students. That means we embed encouraging phrases in our conversation:

- ◆ You can do it.
- ◆ I believe in you.
- ◆ This is a good beginning.
- ◆ I like the way you have done this.
- ◆ This is an interesting perspective

Yet, there are some circumstances in our lives that no amount of encouragement will change. Therefore, in many ways, the classroom becomes the place where many of life's great lessons are learned. One of these lessons is to focus on our talents, not our deficits. For example, a child who lives in poverty may come to school unfamiliar with books, but he may already have skills, such as being able to make change or care for a younger sibling. A child who comes to school who only speaks Spanish has the opportunity to become bilingual. We label these students "at risk" but instead of focusing on the deficits—lack of books or lack of English—we should emphasize the strengths that they possess and build on their assets or their "funds of knowledge" (Scheurich & Skrla, 2003, p. 23). We encourage our students when we emphasize what they *can* do.

Voltaire advised that the most courageous decision "one makes each day is the decision to be in a good mood" (Gorrow, 2004, p. 2). Focusing on the positive fosters a good mood, which is often contagious. A teacher friend of mine was going through a difficult time a few years ago in her personal life. She was thinking of not coming back to teaching the next year because she said it took "too much energy to be positive with the kids." One day she asked her eighth-grade English class to complete a creative writing assignment with the title "The Most Important Thing I Do Every Day." That evening, as she read through the papers, she came to Anne's, a special needs student with debilitating cerebral palsy. It read: "Every single day I get up and choose to focus on the positive things." My friend is still teaching, but with a rekindled spirit.

Because "no pessimist ever discovered the secrets of the stars, or sailed to an uncharted land, or opened a new heaven to the human spirit" (Helen Keller; see http://www.quotationspage.com), we should be optimists and encourage our students to be the same. But we must be realistically optimistic. Jim Collins (2004) recounts the story of General Stockdale, a prisoner of war in Vietnam. General Stockdale pointed out that just being an optimist does not assure success, so when we encourage others, we "must not confuse faith that you will prevail in the end with the discipline to confront...your current reality" (p. 85). In other words, being positive and optimistic without discipline and persistence will accomplish little.

Be Persistent

Herbert Kohl (1994) tells of working with a student who had difficulty talking. He made no progress when he tried to teach the student to read. Over a period of several years, Kohl worked with the boy and tried every trick, technique, and strategy that he knew, but he could not teach him to read. Finally, at 16, the boy learned to read. When Kohl asked him what had happened, even the young man did not know, except that "he decided it was time and so he worked at it" (p. 78). Teachers who don't give up on students keep the spirit alive to continuing trying.

The late musician Ray Charles experienced terrible poverty as a child. He began going blind when he was only 7 or 8 years old. There were many things in his young life that should have kept him from being successful. But he was encouraged in his talent, and he was persistent. The creator of the "Peanuts" comic strip, Charles Schultz, had his drawings rejected over and over, but he believed so strongly in his ability that he kept trying. Johann Sebastian Bach wrote tens of thousands of compositions in his lifetime—enough to fill a 20-foot by 30-foot room, stacked from floor to ceiling. Only five of his compositions were published in his lifetime. Don't ever give up. Mahatma Gandhi offered this reminder to be persistent and persevere no matter what:

It's the action, not the fruit of the action, that's important. You have to do the right thing. It may not be in your power, may not be in your time, that there'll be any fruit. But that doesn't mean you stop doing the right thing. You may never know what results come from your action. But if you do nothing, there will be no result."(Blaydes, 2003, p. 136)

I remember one day when I was teaching my class about origami, the Japanese art of paper folding. Not being particularly crafty or artistic, even with the directions in front of me, I was having difficulty folding my paper into anything recognizable. To extricate myself from this embarrassing failure in front of my students, I was just opening my mouth to say, "Well, I think we've run out of time. We'll come back to this later," when I heard a voice from the back of the classroom say: "Keep trying. You'll get it. Just don't give up." Just like this student, teachers must be persistent in their encouragement of students and of one another.

Provide Resources

A mouse looked through a crack in the wall to see the farmer and his wife opening a package that contained a mousetrap. Frightened, he ran to the farmyard and yelled, "There is a mousetrap in the house!" The chicken clucked and said, "Mr. Mouse, I can tell this is a grave concern to you, but I believe you can handle this." The mouse turned to the pig, who said, "I am so very sorry, Mr. Mouse, but there is nothing I can do about it but pray for you." Then the cow replied, "Really, Mr. Mouse, just keep trying, you'll get rid of it." So the unhappy mouse returned to the house to face the mousetrap alone.

That very night a sound was heard like the sound of a mousetrap catching its prey. The farmer's wife rushed to see what was caught. It was dark and she did not see that it was a venomous snake whose tail the trap had caught. The snake bit the farmer's wife, and she developed a fever. Now everyone knows you treat a fever with fresh chicken soup, so the farmer took his hatchet to the farmyard for the soup's main ingredient.

The wife's sickness continued. So many friends and neighbors came to sit all day and night with her that the farmer had to butcher the pig to feed them all. Then, the farmer's wife died, and even more people came, so that the farmer had the cow slaughtered to provide meat to feed everyone after the funeral (*The Mouse Trap*, 2004).

The moral of this story? The next time you hear that someone has a problem, remember words without resources are useless.

Supportive teachers encourage by being resourceful with supplies, money, and time. If there is no money to buy supplies, teachers never say, "Well, we just won't do that." Instead, we rob our cupboards at home, ask for help from parents, request items from local businesses, and write grants. All the teachers I know spend part of their salary every month on supplies for the classroom—from preschool all the way through to university. Teachers are the only people I know who save milk containers, cereal boxes, box tops, and soup cans, and actually make good use of them!

Asking for resource help from stakeholders extends interest in the school to the larger community, makes connections, and builds relationships that strengthen the school as a learning community. Resourceful teachers organize tutorial times before school in the morning, on their break time, at lunch, and after school. Some teachers come in on Saturday morning to work with students who need extra help. They participate in site-based planning committees to organize and plan ways to meet the resource needs of their students.

I know a college student who lost his job and was living in his truck. One of his teachers heard about this and provided a camper for him to live in until he was able to get a job and rent an apartment. This encouraging act allowed the student who was thinking of dropping out of school to finish the semester, and the following year he earned his degree. When teachers become aware of a need, they do not just offer words of encouragement—they provide resources to meet the need.

Tactical Actions
That Support All Students

What tactical, purposeful actions can teachers implement to build relationships, which value others by being supportive?

- Be visible.
- Be approachable.
- Smile and look pleasant.
- Be honest.
- Speak the truth with tact.
- Make time to listen actively.
- Clarify what is said.
- Recognize students publicly as well as privately.
- Provide parents with ways to communicate with you.
- Visit with parents at school and in their homes.
- Begin with skills that students have mastered to build greater skills.
- Continually assess student progress.
- Notice changes that occur in students.
- Focus on strengths that students have, not so-called deficits.
- Look on the positive side.
- Be realistically optimistic.
- Be persistent.
- Look for new ways to encourage learning.
- Write a grant.
- Make needs known to the community.
- Be available to tutor students.
- Participate in campus planning committees.

When teachers are supportive, they implement actions that communicate effectively and provide encouragement to students, parents, and one another. Even when a student like Kieth seems to be making no progress, teachers cannot give up. Instead, BRAVO teachers must make the most of each moment to rekindle the spirit, time and time again.

Remember, BRAVO teachers build relationships with actions that value others through being supportive.

Actions That Support All Students
Rekindle the Inner Spirit

Support Actions Communicate Effectively
- Be Truthful
- Listen Actively
- Be Available

Support Actions to Encourage
- Build Confidence
- Use Positive Action
- Be Persistent
- Provide Resources

5

Actions That Challenge the Imagination— Participate in Discovery

We can no longer stand at the end of something we visualize in detail and plan backwards from that future. Instead, we must stand at the beginning, clear in our intent, with a willingness to be involved in discovery.

Margaret Wheatley

We were in the lunchroom, and I was helping to collect trays so students could go outside for recess. Suddenly, standing in front of me was a boy, probably about 8 or 9 years old. His hair was red, and his eyes—big and blue—were clouded with tears, which trickled down his freckled cheeks. His name was Scott, and he was clearly miserable. "What's wrong?" I asked. "I just threw my brand new Star Wars watch in the garbage." And then the tears began to roll even faster.

Children in the cafeteria went right on talking, laughing, and eating; and there we stood, next to a trash can filled to overflowing with the remains of a hundred lunches. "Well, maybe, I can help you find it. Are you sure you threw it away?" He sniffled loudly and assured me that he had been in a hurry because his class was already lined up to go outside to play, and without thinking, he threw everything on his tray in the trash can, lined up with his class, and only then remembered that his watch had been on his tray. His *new Star Wars watch!* He had wanted it for ages, he said, sobbing.

What could I do? I rolled up my sleeves and began digging in the garbage. While Scott watched, the tears began to recede and were replaced with a look of hope. "Please, Lord, let her find it." He didn't say this aloud, but I could read his thoughts.

Well, there was no watch in the top layer—perhaps a little lower. Yuck, it was getting pretty messy. I used to love refried beans, but they kept sticking to my fingers, and oh no! Now I had little pieces of orange, chili-soaked rice under my finger nails. I thought I might be sick.

"Now, you're sure you threw it in the garbage?" Uh oh, here came the tears again. "Yes, ma'am, it was right on the edge of my tray—my brand new Star Wars watch." With a sigh, I plunged my hand deeper into the garbage again, and leaned over with my head and my nose (oh, no, those smells!) closer to the garbage so I could see better. I stood up—not giving up—just trying to recover my equilibrium. I took another deep breath before plunging back into the mess.

Then, all of a sudden, on a whim, I stuck my garbage-laden hand into his jacket pocket and pulled out—a brand new Star Wars watch!

Although my experience with Scott might not seem particularly inspiring, it taught me a valuable lesson: If you are not finding what you are looking for, or if things are not working as you had hoped, despite what everyone says, try something different—challenge your imagination to participate in discovery.

We all know teachers who put up the same bulletin boards every year, use the same lesson plans, and even set up their classrooms in the very same way. These teachers have only one experience, but they have it 10, 15, or maybe even 20 times! Despite the needs of children in their classroom, they are so tied to doing things the way they have always done them, that there is no room to try anything different. I actually knew a second-grade teacher who really did use her lesson plans, the *exact* same lesson plans, from year to year. One year a new principal came to the school, and he moved teachers to different grade levels. Within a month she resigned.

To be open to change, we must be flexible. I'm reminded of how difficult it is to be flexible when I remember something my daughter did as a first grader when she went through the lunch line for the first time at school. When the ladies working in the cafeteria asked her what dressing she wanted on her salad, she replied very importantly in her best 6-year-old voice that she would have "the house dressing, please." It's been 25 years since that happened, and when I see these ladies today, they still ask about my "inflexible" daughter.

Did you know that there are 293 ways to make change for a dollar? Sometimes teachers must "unlearn old beliefs to learn new, more productive ones in order to successfully teach [children]" (Scheurich & Skrla, 2003, p. 52). However, to do this we must activate our imaginations to be open to change, be willing to find new ways to solve problems creatively, and be able to manage conflict. When we participate in this kind of discovery we enrich ourselves and our classrooms with actions that build valuing relationships with our students, parents, and other teachers.

Challenge the Imagination with Actions That Are Open to Change

Change is a constant. The world is changing so rapidly that Peter Senge wrote that schools used to teach as much as 80% of what students needed to know; now it is only 2%. More than 80% of items we see on the grocery shelves did not even exist in 1940! When I was a first-year teacher, I don't believe the word "latchkey" child had even been coined, yet today there are more than 12 million latchkey children between the ages of 6 and 13. Think back to your first year as a teacher. Assuming that was at least 10 years ago, what changes have you noticed in the world? Today, most of your teacher friends have laptops; e-mail is a major form of communication with parents; surfing the Internet is a major part of how you plan lessons; everyone has a cell phone (even many of the students); grades are entered on a computer program; and copies are made by a scanner electronically or by Xerox machines that make 100 copies in less than a minute. In my first year as a teacher, I used a Smith-Corona typewriter with carbon paper to make a duplicate; communicated with parents usually by telephone or by writing letters and mailing them with 10-cent stamps; surfing was something that was done in California that the Beach Boys sang about;, to use the telephone I went to the office after school; grades were entered by hand in a grade book; and I made copies using a mimeograph machine, and when I finished, I was as purple as the ink on the copies. Making 100 copies would have taken forever.

If you are a new teacher, ask your parents to describe what the world was like when they were in high school. And if you are still not convinced that the world is a place of change, ask your grandmother or grandfather the same question. There is only one thing that is probably quite the same, and that is how we teach school. Even though today we have computers in most of our classrooms, teachers still teach in much the same way. Students sit in neat rows; the class rules are placed on the wall; we write assignments on a white board rather than on a chalkboard; and most students spend much of their school day listening to teachers. But if teachers are going to teach all students successfully, we will need to be open to change, for "life requires that we change. It cannot explore new possibilities otherwise" (Wheatley & Keller-Rogers, 1999, p. 33).

Change is about people and people "engage in change only as we discover that we might be more of who we are by becoming something different" (Wheatley & Kellner-Rogers, 1999, p. 50). Although we tend to emphasize that change is for everyone else, the truth is that change must begin with each of us. Being open to change means we realize that things are not always as they seem, we must develop different perspectives, and we must be willing to take risks. Being open to change is invitational; it invites teachers to build valuing relationships with students, parents, and faculty members.

Realize That Things Are Not Always as They Seem

I was in my car driving the other day when I looked up and saw an airplane above the city preparing to land. It appeared to be hanging suspended in the sky and not moving at all. I looked again, and it still hung there looking as though it had not moved even an inch, yet I knew that it was probably traveling at least 200 miles per hour. Things are not always as they seem.

If you have ever been to East Texas, you would have found that the highway was lined with beautiful, tall pine trees that stretch regally to the skies. Their always-green limbs sway gracefully with the wind. One Saturday, February 1, 2003, I was driving from Nacogdoches, Texas, to Houston to catch a plane to fly to my home in San Antonio. The day was sunny, and as I drove I remember thinking that it was going to be a lovely day. Suddenly, my cell phone rang. It was my mother, and she was upset, asking if I was all right. I said that I was fine, but why was she worried? She had been listening to the news, and at that very moment as I was driving casually, admiring the scenery, and enjoying the day, the space shuttle Columbia had exploded nearly 40 miles above the earth and was falling in pieces onto East Texas. Things are not always as they seem.

Robert was an 11-year-old boy in my class. He was one of those children who made me question my commitment to teaching. His attendance was poor, there was little parent support, and although capable, his work was always poorly done, if done at all. He was argumentative and loud, in class and on the playground. I hate to admit this, but to be honest, when he was absent from school, I often breathed a sigh of relief knowing that the school day would be much better since he was not there to disrupt. I saw Robert as an angry, difficult, and irresponsible adolescent. One day during a creative free-writing assignment, he actually turned in a completed paper. This is the story he wrote:

> Said the little boy, "Sometimes I drop my spoon."
>
> Said the little, old man, "I do that, too."
>
> The little boy said, "I wet my pants."
>
> "I do that too," said the little, old man.
>
> Said the little boy, "I often cry."
>
> The old man nodded, "So do I."
>
> "But worst of all," said the boy, "It seems, grownups don't pay attention to me."
>
> And he felt the warmth of a withered old hand.
>
> "I know what you mean," said the little, old man.

Sometimes things are not always as they seem. When I read this, I knew that Robert was not who he seemed to be. I was the teacher, I had to be open to change and try harder to know more about him. Life happens in many dimensions, and teachers who build valuing relationships with students teach with a heightened awareness and sensitivity to what seems to be and what is.

Develop Different Perspectives

We often make the mistake of thinking that everyone thinks just as we do. But this is not so. Maturana and Varela (1992) explain that what we see is "most influenced by who we have decided to be" (p. 49). In fact, they tell us that what we see with our eyes only accounts for 20% of how we create perception, and the other 80% that affects our perception is information that is already in the brain. Just ask two children about something that happened in the classroom. You will likely get two different answers. In fact, if you ask three or four children, you will probably get that many different perceptions of what occurred. While this is a frustrating problem for teachers, it clearly suggests that there is more than one way of looking at an issue.

There is rarely just one answer to most concerns; rather there are usually several possible answers—all of which are appropriate. Consider the Indian tale of the blind men and the elephant. The man who felt the animal's side described it as being like a strong wall. The man who felt its tusk described the elephant like a spear. The third man felt around the elephant's leg and described it like a tree. The fourth man reached up and touched the elephant's ear, then noted that it was actually like a fan. The fifth man grabbed the animal's tail and considered it was like a rope. The sixth man felt the elephant's trunk and insisted that it was like a large snake! All were right, but none were completely right. Developing a different perspective provides teachers with enhanced possibilities for change.

Teachers who are imaginative and willing to change develop different perspectives about students and about learning. The world is changing rapidly all around us. We should be preparing our students to live in a world where information itself is changing every day. Often technology is at the center of this. For example, when I first began teaching, computers in the schools were simply unheard of. Today they are a necessity.

Today, when I think back on my early years of teaching, I'm sorry that I spent so much time having students memorize countries of the world, many of which no longer exist. I wish instead I had spent more time helping them learn how to read a map. I wish I hadn't spent so much time teaching them to memorize the capital cities of Europe and Asia. I wish instead I had worked with them to better understand some of the worldwide cultures and how we are alike and how we are different. The world is so much smaller today. I was 40 before I ever went to another country other than Mexico, but my own daughter had been to Europe three times before she was 25. I have friends today who live in such faraway places as the Ukraine and Kazakhstan. Just as the world is changing, today's students need teachers who are willing to change old teaching patterns and strategies to better prepare them to live in this changing world.

Changing our perspective about parents is an example of beliefs that may need to change for some of us. There is an American Indian saying that to understand someone we "should walk a mile in their moccasins." Of course, the modern version of that adds "That way, when you do criticize them, you are a mile away and you have their shoes (Blaydes, 2003, p. 128). Seriously, though, seeing something from another person's perspective encourages empathy, which allows us to feel what others are feeling. I often hear teachers complain that some parents don't care about their children because they don't come to PTA meetings or help their children the way a teacher thinks they should (I may have said this once or twice myself!). But if we knew more about our students' parents and their particular situations, understood that things may not be as they seem, and were willing to look with a different perspective, we most likely would realize that we were being unwisely judgmental. The truth is no one loves their children more than parents, regardless of what we might think. We change our beliefs when we enlarge our perspective. Changing our beliefs to include broader perspectives is a positive step toward building valuing relationships.

Risk Thinking Differently

When we are open to change, we acknowledge that things are not always as they seem, and we develop a different perspective about students and about teaching itself. In this process we become more willing to risk thinking differently and trying new strategies in our classrooms. Reviewing data is an important strategy that makes it easier for teachers to be open to change.

A few years ago, a teacher friend worked in a high school with a well-respected reputation in a suburban community. A new industry was built in the area that brought in workers with lower-paying jobs. Inexpensive apartments were built in the school's attendance zone. The school population became much more diverse. Still, the school scored well on the standardized tests that were given, and the advanced placement classes stayed full. When a new principal came to the school, he asked teachers to meet with him voluntarily to review achievement scores in depth. Only three teachers came to the meeting (my friend was one of them). The other teachers felt that the scores showed that the school was doing fine and that it was just not necessary to spend their time reviewing the test scores. The principal and the committee of three teachers got to work. In reviewing the data, they discovered that scores of the Caucasian students were actually higher than they had been in previous years. They also discovered that the scores for the students who had transferred in because of the new company were low, and none of these students were enrolled in the AP classes.

The principal pondered what to do. Finally, the small committee of teachers spoke up. They liked and respected the other teachers, but they knew that there would be strong resistance to any sort of change that might be proposed. To make a long story short, on the advice of the committee, he required all faculty members to meet during the next professional development day. He divided them into small groups and provided each group with the data available. He gave only two instructions: Review the data carefully and make a plan based on the data for us to consider. Each teacher group came up with the same recommendation on their own: We need to do something differently to support our new students—they are not doing well at all. The word *change* was never used, but when faced with the data they were able to risk thinking differently.

Be willing to risk never playing the blame game. No one is more likely to participate in bringing about change to your school just because of being blamed for something that did not work. The blame game causes people to react personally.

As a teacher, your interest is what is best for the students that you teach right now. Therefore, blaming last year's teacher for a student's failure is just not acceptable under any circumstances. Your job is to move students forward from where they are today. Playing the blame game is of no value to anyone interested in creating change.

Today, as I write this chapter, there is an article in the newspaper about a school where teachers and the principal were cheating by giving students the answers on the high-stakes tests that Texas mandates. In every case, the teachers and the principal played the blame game and blamed their actions on the stress and the importance of the test. Not one of them accepted the blame for making an unethical decision to cheat, nor did they accept the blame for participating. Not one of them said, "If we had just kept our focus on what is best for the kids, we would have put our energies into teaching them well rather than wasting our time on cheating." BRAVO (Building Relationships with Actions that Value Others) teachers risk thinking differently. If we make a mistake, we accept the blame, correct it, and move forward.

Challenge the Imagination by Solving Problems Creatively

Solving problems is a challenge to every teacher. Solving problems creatively is an even greater challenge. Most of us solve problems for immediacy by assigning consequences to students rather than looking for long-term improvement. Creative problem solving reminds me of a story. The children were lined up in the cafeteria of a parochial elementary school for lunch. At the head of the table was a large pile of apples. The nun made a note and posted it on the apple tray: "Take only ONE. God is watching." Moving further along the lunch line, at the other end of the table was a large pile of chocolate chip cookies. A child had written a note: "Take all you want, God is watching the apples." Creative problem solving!

Seriously though, problems never go away—instead they grow. So, our goal in problem solving should be finding solutions that are lasting. The philosopher Schopenhauer suggested that "the task is not so much to see what no one yet has seen, but to think what nobody yet has thought about that which everybody sees" (Wheatley & Kellner-Rogers, 1999, p. i). Sometimes creative problem solving is right before our eyes, but we have to think differently and ask for help, acknowledge our mistakes, and consider conflicts as learning opportunities.

Ask for Help

Belinda was a 10-year-old third grader with strawberry-blonde hair, an always-dirty blouse, and ill-fitting clothes. She never sat still, and she smelled bad. She was in my class the second year I taught school. One minute Belinda would come up to me, sucking on her thumb, and give me a hug. The next minute, she would kick and scream that she did not like me at all. During a spelling test, Belinda would erupt and shout out the spelling of the words. On the playground she would go from group to group begging someone to play with her. Occasionally, a compassionate third grader would allow her to play, only to have the game disrupted within minutes by Belinda's screaming, yelling, and tears. At the end of the day, I often went home in tears. What was I doing wrong? Why couldn't I help Belinda control herself?

Belinda's parents would not come in for a conference. "We can't even get her to take a bath at home or go to sleep at night; How can we possibly help you?" they told me in a frustrated telephone call. So, I looked at her school records. Since preschool, she had been a problem. Thinking that she was just immature, she had been retained once. Her previous teachers gave this advice, "Hang in there, the year will be over, eventually." When I asked how they had coped with her, they all said, "Finally, I just ignored her."

But I was Belinda's teacher, and I could not just ignore her. But, how could I, a new teacher, help her, when veteran teachers had failed completely to bring about any change? I tried charts; I tried rewards; I read everything I could find on disruptive children; I went to my principal for advice. I needed help. The school psychologist came to observe. He came back again and again. He expressed shock and anger that this child was 10 years old and no one had sought professional help for her before. There was no doubt that she needed help desperately.

Sometimes, after we have tried and tried to solve problems by ourselves, we must admit, not that we have failed, but that we need help. The help Belinda needed was there all the time, I just had to ask for it.

Acknowledge Mistakes as Learning Opportunities

When Thomas Edison was 67 years old, his laboratory was almost completely destroyed by fire. He had very little insurance, and the damage exceeded 2 million dollars. Much of his life's work went up in flames that night. The next morning, Edison looked at the ashes and remarked, "There is great value in disaster. All our mistakes are burned up. Thank God we can start anew." Three weeks later, Edison managed to deliver his first phonograph (Canfield & Hansen, 1996).

Unfortunately, rather than learning from our mistakes, too often our tendency is to sweep them under the carpet and try to forget that they ever happened. But acknowledging our mistakes is a powerful aspect of problem solving when we are willing to learn. In fact, educator Anne Wilson Schaef said that "we don't make mistakes, we just have learnings" (www.educationquotes.com). Isaac Asimov must have considered learning from our mistakes a key to discovery, when he said, "The most exciting phrase to hear in science, the one that heralds new discoveries, is not 'Eureka! I've found it!', but 'That's funny....'" (www.educationquotes.com).

When teachers openly acknowledge mistakes, whether it is to students, parents, or faculty members, we model an important character builder for students: accepting responsibility for an error and using it as a learning opportunity. I'll never forget one of my first mistakes in the classroom. I had put up with Jackie's antics all year long—he was just ornery, but somehow I had maintained my temper and had never blown up (visibly, anyway). Finally, it was the last day of the school year. In fact, it was the last hour. He did something (I have no idea what it was now), but all of a sudden, I just lost it! I raised my voice, I yelled at him and all of the others who were not doing whatever they were supposed to be doing right then. I ranted forever, it seems. I waved my arms. Yes, I had a tantrum, right there in front of all my students, on the last day and the last few minutes that we would ever be together. I blew it!

Finally, I shut up. I looked at my students who were now sitting in their chairs like silent robots, not moving a muscle. You could have heard a pin drop; it was that quiet. My students were in shock—they had never seen this side of me, and they did not know what to do. Immediately, I was just sick. I couldn't believe that I had reacted like that, over nothing really. But it was the last day of the school year, and the day had been quite unstructured, and I was tired, and they were tired, and—no excuses. I had just made a colossal mistake. There was only one thing to do. I swallowed my pride, looked at Jackie, and said, "Jackie, I am so sorry, please forgive me for losing my patience like that." Then I looked at my class and said, "I really lost it, didn't I? Please forgive me, I am very sorry." Within minutes, I was getting hugs from 20 very forgiving and relieved third graders.

If we are going to encourage students that mistakes are important ways for us to learn, they need to see us acknowledge our mistakes, learn from them, and move on. (I learned that if I could hold my temper for 179 days, I could certainly hold it for 180 days!) R. Buckminster Fuller said, "If I ran a school, I'd give the average grades to the ones who gave me all the right answers, for being good parrots. I'd give the top grades to those who made a lot of mistakes and told me about them, and then told me what they learned from them" (www.educationquotes.com).

Consider Conflict a Learning Opportunity

Conflict, when dealt with creatively, is a catalyst to solving problems. Of course, this means that we must not react emotionally or take issues personally. Instead, teachers must respond thoughtfully and listen carefully. Conflict can actually provide a powerful source of information about students because sometimes the only way you will get to know many of your parents is when there is a conflict that is serious enough for parents to contact you. So, look on the bright side. Conflict generally provides an opportunity for communication—it's up to you, however, to turn it into a constructive opportunity for communication.

When I first began teaching, several experienced teachers suggested strategies for dealing with conflict quickly. One told me that when something happened at school, such as when a child got in trouble or fell on the playground and bumped his head, and I felt it was serious enough that he would go home and tell his parents, that I should always make the first contact. In other words, I should telephone the parent before the child got home from school to alert them about what had happened. This was great advice. First of all, the parents liked knowing what happened rather than being surprised when their child came home. When the child got home and shared what happened from their perspective, parents were able to balance this with the information I had given them earlier. This strategy usually kept me from receiving an angry phone call and also provided a good opportunity to get to know parents better. If parents did call, it was usually to clarify something or give me additional information, but it was rarely a conflict call.

Another piece of advice I was given that first year was to tell my students that if something (anything) happened at school that made them unhappy or hurt them, they should tell me about it. In other words, if students thought whatever happened was important enough to tell their parents, they must be sure that I knew about it first. After all, I was there to help them, and I couldn't do my job if I did not have all the information. This time, I was the one who appreciated not being surprised. If a parent did call about a concern, I was able to talk about it without having to say, "Gee, I had no idea that happened." I firmly believe that many conflicts were averted simply by addressing them early.

I also learned that when parents were angry with me, the best thing to do was to listen very carefully to their concerns before I attempted to say anything. When I responded, I would restate their concerns using their words when I could remember them (it helps to take notes while they talk). Then the conversation might have gone something like this:

> Teacher: "So, Johnny said that I embarrassed him when I raised my voice at him for being out of his seat when the guest speaker was talking."
>
> Angry parent: "Yes, that's right. How dare you embarrass my son like that."
>
> Teacher: "I apologize for embarrassing him. That was not my intent. The children needed to be able to hear our speaker."
>
> Angry parent: "Well, I can understand that, but you shouldn't embarrass my son."
>
> Teacher: "Of course, you are right. It's never my intent to embarrass any child. Can I help you with anything else?"
>
> Angry parent: "No, it's okay."
>
> Teacher: "Well, thank you for coming in and bringing this to my attention. I hope that you will always feel comfortable to share your concerns with me"

Often the conflict was minimized fairly rapidly by listening. Then the conflict was reduced further by my willingness to apologize for embarrassing the child. Some of you are probably saying, "I can't believe you apologized!" Of course, I should have apologized for embarrassing the child. Teachers should never embarrass a child, and if we do, no matter how unintentional, we should apologize. Even the great Winston Churchill apologized from time to time and said that "Eating words has never given me indigestion." Humility goes a long way in building relationships with students and parents. Notice that in this particular scenario, I did not apologize for asking him to be seated. Also, notice that by responding this way, the door was opened for a future relationship with the parent, which should always be one of our goals. By the way, this particular incident really did happen almost verbatim, and that parent became one of my strongest supporters. A few weeks later, she actually came to me and apologized for *her* anger on that day.

Don't misunderstand what I am saying. I do not enjoy conflict, and often I would come home from school, the phone would ring, and I wanted to pretend that I never heard it. Many times I did not want to meet with an angry parent face to face. But a wise mentor teacher told me early on to remember one thing when dealing with unhappy parents: "No matter how much you care about a child in your class, the parents love the child far more… so listen to them and discover all you can about the child. You will be a stronger teacher for it." She was right.

Much of teacher time is spent responding to problems, so creativity is important. One way we become more creative is to quit being fearful of being wrong. Actions that challenge our imagination help us solve problems creatively. When we ask for help, acknowledge mistakes, and consider conflict as learning opportunities. We solve problems, but in the process we build relationships that value others.

Tactical Actions That Challenge the Imagination

What tactical actions that challenge the imagination can teachers implement that build relationships that value others?

- ♦ Be open to new ways of doing things.
- ♦ Differentiate how someone (something) seems from what he or she (it) may really be.
- ♦ Recognize that there are more ways than one to solve problems.
- ♦ Think outside the box.
- ♦ Consider other perspectives.
- ♦ Ask for help.
- ♦ Risk trying something new.
- ♦ Ask "what if?"
- ♦ Ask "why not?"

- Ask "why is that?"
- Deal with problems quickly.
- Don't take conflict personally.
- Listen and then speak.
- Don't play the blame game.

When teachers make the most of each moment to challenge the imagination and look at the world with a different set of eyes, they become open to immense possibilities in a rapidly changing world, and solving problems becomes a creative endeavor. The Russian Cosmonaut Krikalev left Leningrad for a 313-day journey in space in 1991. He returned almost a year later to discover that his city was no longer on the map, and his country no longer existed (Blaydes, 2003, p. 77). Most of us participate in much smaller discoveries, such as finding a child's watch, but we also "become an explorer with the goal of uncovering or helping [our] students uncover the gifts and strengths that can nurture them as they grow" (Kohl, 1994, p. 79). These kinds of actions build relationships that value others.

Remember, BRAVO teachers build relationships that value others by challenging the imagination.

Actions that Challenge the Imagination

Participate in Discovery

**Challenge the Imagination with Actions
That Are Open to Change**

- Realize That Things Are Not Always as They Seem
- Develop Different Perspectives
- Risk Thinking Differently

Solve Problems Creatively

- Ask for Help
- Acknowledge Mistakes as Learning Opportunities
- Consider Conflict a Learning Opportunity

6

Actions That Demonstrate Culturally Responsive Teaching—The Mosaic of Moral Purpose

Mother Culture, whose voice has been in your ear since the day of your birth, has given you an explanation of how things came to be this way. You know it well; everyone in your culture knows it well. But this explanation wasn't give to you all at once. No one ever sat you down and said, "Here is how things came to be this way, beginning ten or fifteen billion years ago right up to the present." Rather, you assembled this explanation like a mosaic: from a million bits of information, presented to you in various ways by others who share that explanation.

Quinn (1992, p. 40)

Hector and Maria walked haltingly into my remedial reading class one day in the early 1970s. Hector was strong and tall for his age. Maria was much slighter than her brother, although they shared the same features. They had just moved to my city from Mexico. They spoke no English, and I spoke no Spanish. Every day they walked, holding hands, into my remedial reading class for a reading lesson.

Hector and Maria always smiled. When they appeared at the doorway of my classroom, they would both nod at me and smile, as though asking for permission to enter. I would smile back and welcome them. They would go straight to their assigned task—still smiling. When we read together, they both made valiant efforts—always smiling. When either of them made a mistake, both would look at each other knowingly and smile, say "Okay," and continue to read the unfamiliar English words. Within a few days, they were speaking all kinds of English phrases, and I was trying just as diligently, although without the same success, to learn some Spanish phrases from them. Every day I looked forward to seeing Hector and Maria, smiling and holding hands, walk into my classroom.

One day they did not come. The next day they were also absent. By the third day, I became concerned and checked on them in the school office. Where were they? No one knew. Hector and Maria, I remember them—brother and sister, holding hands, smiling, trying to learn to read a language they did not speak.

Now, years later, there are so many things that I wish I had done for Hector and Maria in the short time they were in my class. But at the time I was young and had little knowledge of any culture other than my own white, middle-class, midwest upbringing. I doubt that I had even given a thought to how culture influenced my own beliefs and actions. There was just so much that I did not know. Looking back, I am sure they knew that I cared about them, but I don't know if I helped them at all in the challenges that lay before them in their new land.

Since that time, major changes have occurred in the United States regarding diversity, particularly in race and economics. For example, according to Hodgkinson (2003), between 2001 and 2015, 48 states (not Arkansas and Mississippi) are expected to have increases in their minority populations. In 2000, about 65% of U.S. school-age children were non-Hispanic whites, and by 2020 this number is expected to drop to 56%. By 2015, in California, Texas, Florida, and New York, minority students will become the majority.

The United States is still the richest nation in terms of gross national product, but the gap between rich and poor is increasing. Of the 73,000,000 children under age 18 who live in the United States, 17% live in poverty. Of these children, 9% are white, 32% are black, 29% are Latino, 12% are Asian, and 35% are American Indian. Eight percent of teenagers are dropouts. Of these, 6% are white, 10% are black, 5% are Asian, 10% are American Indian, and 17% are Latino. Additionally, the number of students who speak a language other than English at home has more than doubled since 1979 from 6.3 million to 13.7 million in 1999 (Kids Count, 2004).

These changing demographics of racial and economic trends take on serious implications when we consider that at present while almost 40% of our students are nonwhite, only 10% of secondary teachers, 14% of K–6 teachers, 16% of principals, and only 4% of superintendents are nonwhite (Hodgkinson, 2003). In other words, as our students become more and more diverse, considering racial and economic trends, educators are becoming less diverse.

Black and Latino students have become more segregated in impoverished school districts than at any time in the last 30 years. The segregation of white students is so pronounced that it occurs even within majority black and Latino school districts (Fears, 2001). Consequently, as our students become more and more diverse, they attend schools that are becoming less diverse.

We live today in a world where the clash of cultures resounds loudly. What should be a lovely mosaic of diversity often looks instead like a confusing, chaotic splash of color on canvas without design. We are more diverse, yet in many ways and many places, we are more separate. The world of post–9/11 is like that canvas, confusing and chaotic, but understanding the importance of culture helps teachers build valuing relationships with the opportunity to create something of beauty. As culturally responsive teachers, we are committed to the moral purpose of helping all children achieve in our schools. In this way, according to Brazilian educator, Paulo Freire, we empower learners to become "dreamers of possible utopias" (1998, p. 45).

Culture, which shapes what we are as well as what we think, is seen as multilayered elements of life transmitted from generation to generation. Pang (2005) breaks these elements into three layers:

♦ Ways we communicate—language, proverbs, jokes, stories, holidays

♦ Ways we interact—verbal tone of voice, nonverbal communication patterns (eye contact, proximity), family behaviors, gender roles

♦ What we value—attitudes, values, spiritual beliefs, fears, laws, standards, expectations

In order for teacher actions to be culturally responsive, we must be willing to confront our own biases, as well as those that exist in the classroom. Having done this, we acknowledge and affirm cultural diversity in our students' lives and integrate this knowledge into the classroom. This leads us to become more than bridge builders; instead we should be about crossing bridges. As teachers do this, we build relationships that value others.

Confront Personal Biases

All of us have biases. We don't like to admit it and some of us never do—but in truth, we all have prejudices. We are all guilty of stereotyping people from mothers-in-law to Texans. I remember one Christmas, my husband, daughter, and I were in New York City. One evening, we went to a comedy club on Broadway. During the comedian's monologue, he began talking to the audience. He looked directly at us and said, "Well, I see that we have three Texans over here." Then he said, "Only Texans wear sweaters with sequined Christmas trees on the front." My daughter and I looked at each other. Sure enough, we were wearing sweaters with sequined Christmas trees on the front! He may have been guilty of stereotyping, but I can assure you that neither of us has ever worn a sweater with sequined Christmas trees since!

However, most of the time stereotyping is a reflection of deeply held prejudices, and it causes much pain. In a recent doctoral class that I taught, one of my students, an outstanding young man who is a high school principal in Louisiana, shared a frustrating experience that happens often to him. It is not unusual for him to see white women lock their car doors when they see him crossing the street, even in broad daylight. He is a tall, young African American.

I had just flown in to Portland, Oregon, a city that I had never visited before. I got on the monorail, which would take me downtown. I pulled out a map to see if I could figure out how to get to my hotel. The young man sitting across from me was dressed all in black, his hair was long, and he was tattooed and had numerous body piercings. He leaned over to ask if I needed help. I immediately moved away from him. Realizing what I had done, I swallowed and said, "You know I really don't know where I am going. Do you know the city?" For the next few minutes that we were on the monorail, he gave me directions, then talked about some of the great things to see in the city. He was a delightful young man, whom I had almost misjudged when I shouldn't have been judging at all.

Last year, on our way back from Ireland, we were flying to Houston. The plane landed in Chicago and everyone had to deplane, go through customs, and then those who were continuing on to Houston had to collect their luggage, check it again, and reboard the plane. As we waited for our luggage, I noticed a Muslim woman dressed in black with a hijab (scarf) covering her head. She was struggling with her luggage, so I asked if she would like some help. As we began to visit, she turned to me with tears in her eyes and said, "I have lived in Chicago since I was a child—for over 40 years. When we went through customs, I noticed the agent welcomed you back to the United States. When I went through, he said nothing. This is my country, too!"

We must not fool ourselves, prejudice resides in each of us; it is everywhere. Unfortunately, we hold biases that include the way people look; how they dress; and their size, gender, ethnicity, age, handicapping conditions, academic achievement ability, sexual preference, socioeconomic status, level of schooling, job, and language. Sometimes, we are not aware that we even have these beliefs until we spend time in candid self-examination.

Despite the fact that most of us who talk about caring, love, peace, and respect for all believe in these moral values, the sad truth is that hate and bitter prejudice do exist. A recent issue of *Newsweek* magazine told of a CD company that sells "white power" music. This group was planning a project called Project Schoolyard, which would distribute 100,000 free CDs. The website boasted that "We don't just entertain racist kids, we create them" (Childress & Johnson, 2004, p. 32). One of the young people in this article pointed out how good it made him feel when he realized that "there were [other] angry kids like him—angry at blacks, Jews, homosexuals, immigrants...."

We have a moral obligation as teachers to examine ourselves, identify, and rid ourselves of prejudice and bias. Nor can we waste time feeling guilty when we recognize mistakes that we have made in the past. Guilt serves no purpose, but growing does. Until I spent time examining and identifying my own biases, I didn't know what beliefs I needed to change. Now I do. Until I began to understand where I really stood on important issues like "respect for all" and "appreciating diversity," I rarely talked about these issues, particularly racial issues. I was afraid that I would hurt someone's feelings or say the wrong thing. Then, about six years ago, teaching a university class of future principals, the only black student in the class noted that he rarely went outside at night. When I asked why, he shared at length. When he finished talking, I realized for the first time that I had to take my head out of the sand and look at things as they really are. I realized the incredible importance of being openly antiracist and antiprejudiced; not to *convince* others to believe exactly what I believe, but to begin the dialogue about our experiences so that we can grow together.

What are some things that I do now? I make a point of smiling at people, especially people who do *not* look like me; I have become more friendly, and I actually talk to people even if they do *not* look like me; I make sure that my actions are affirming and welcoming; I do not laugh at jokes that denigrate others; I have become more inclusive in all of my actions; and I bring the dialogue to school and share the importance of recognizing biases at every opportunity with my students and other faculty members. And this is only the beginning, I am still learning. Otherwise we remain blind to what our students can plainly see.

Confront Biases in the Classroom

The same biases exist in the classroom too. Parents come to the PTA meeting and we spend our time talking with the wealthy parents and saying little to other parents. Little Janey's father is a doctor; we invite him in to talk in science class. Angie's father is a farmer, but we don't invite him to speak even though he has vast knowledge of plants.

A young man in one of my principal classes wrote a research paper last year on students who were goths. He interviewed several of these boys and girls. Nearly all of them commented that they felt ostracized by their teachers. Another one of my students shared that her 12-year-old son, who is part Latino and part Arabic, confronts prejudice daily at school because of his mixed race. Now, after 9/11 it is much worse. He is reluctant to talk to the teacher because she will just think I am "being a baby." Teachers tell me that they frequently get calls from parents asking them to move their children from a table because their tablemate is a different ethnicity.

Consistently, we equate difference with deficit. Marlee Matlan, the actress, is deaf. She tells of a time when she was on an airplane looking at the dinner menu. When the flight attendant realized she was deaf, she grabbed the menu from her hand and brought her one—in Braille. When I mentioned this to one of my university classes, someone pointed out that a similar incident occurred with a group of deaf students at a fast-food restaurant. When the person behind the counter realized the students were deaf, they were given menus in Braille. Difference is NOT deficit!

In the work that I do on peer harassment in schools, I consistently hear of students being bullied, painfully teased, or made fun of because they are different—gay, poor, too short, too tall, do not dress well, and on and on. Less than 10% of students who are bullied report to their teachers, counselors, or administrators that they are being mistreated because they don't feel that teachers will or can do anything about it, or they feel that we don't care.

Joshua Aronson (2004) and his colleague Claude Steele have studied how students cope with unflattering stereotypes and refer to it as *stereotype threat*. They found that this has a powerful effect in the relatively poor achievement of African Americans, Latinos, and girls in math-oriented domains. They report that children as young as 6 years are aware of cultural stereotypes, that stereotypes are widely believed, and that about half of white Americans agree with common stereotyping of blacks and Latinos as unintelligent.

I remember something that happened the very first year that I taught school. Connie was 10 years old. She was the smallest girl in the class. I still remember her yellow-gold curls that moved gently when she walked. Her skin was fair, and her eyes were blue. She was always dressed perfectly in matching everything. Connie talked a lot in class, usually without raising her hand or asking for permission.

One day I asked the students to make a circle. Connie was standing next to James. James was tall, skinny, and African American. His clothes were hand-me-downs—on the third or fourth trip down. He had an opinion about everything—especially about Martin Luther King, his hero. I asked the children to join hands. Connie refused to take James's hand. I looked at her thinking, "Oh no, here we go again with the 'boy-girl' thing—she won't take his hand because he's a boy."

Just as I started to say something, Connie looked at me and said loudly for everyone to hear: "I won't hold James's hand 'cause he's black and dirty." The room became silent. My heart stopped, and I looked immediately at James who hugged his hand to himself, and, for a moment, his eyes looked ashamed. I recovered from my shock and walked over to James and firmly took his hand in mine, my other hand reached out to Connie. It was at that moment that I realized that teachers are often the bridge that brings diverse groups together. We do this by building relationships with our students and their parents that value them as individuals.

Acknowledge and Affirm Cultural Diversity

One year, I worked with an instructional aide who had come to the United States from Mexico in 1950, when she was 12 years old. Of course, at that time, she had spoken only Spanish, but her parents wanted her to learn English and do well in school. So, the first week they were in the United States, they walked her proudly to school, and she enrolled in a local junior high. School was a frustrating experience for her. She was not allowed to speak any Spanish. There were other girls in her class who spoke Spanish, but they had lived here longer and also spoke English now. Her teachers spoke no Spanish. She hoped that the teachers would let her new friends translate, but that was not allowed. She was very confused. When recess came, she was relieved and ran eagerly onto the playground. One of the other girls came up to her, and they began speaking in Spanish. When the teacher realized what they were doing, she was brought inside and made to sit in the classroom by herself until recess was over. She survived, learned to speak English, and eventually graduated from high school. But when she told me about this, 25 years had gone by, and she still cried.

When I first began teaching, there was little discussion of multiculturalism and none of diversity or culturally responsive classrooms. Instead, the prevailing thought when dealing with different ethnic groups was that everyone should blend into the melting pot and just be American. In other words, we should *not* recognize ethnic or other cultural differences at all. We would just be one big happy family—all alike. Of course, that meant that our curriculum was almost completely Euro-

centric. I can remember saying proudly on more than one oc-
casion, "Oh, I couldn't even tell you what ethnicity students
are in my class. I don't even notice." This was done with good
intentions, but by *not* noticing cultural diversity, it was as
though we were saying it was bad—as though we equated *diversity* with *deficit*.

Today, just as I am older and, hopefully, wiser, our education system is older and wiser—at least in this regard. Instead
of ignoring cultural diversity, we now acknowledge that it exists, seek to understand it better, and affirm its presence as an
asset to be cherished in the lives of our students and their
families.

Last year, a graduate student from Kazakhstan spent a
year at our university. I invited her to come home to visit my
city and stay with me for a week. The first morning when I
came downstairs to fix breakfast, she was sitting at the breakfast table waiting for me. In her hand was a baggie filled with
pancakes. She had brought her breakfast for the week with
her. She later explained to me that in Kazakhstan, food is
scarce, and when you visit someone, you always take your
own food, so that your visit will not be a hardship on the host
family. Because our world has become smaller in many ways,
we must be sensitive to the unique beliefs and behaviors that
are grounded in cultural influence.

BRAVO (Building Relationships with Actions that Value
Others) teachers explore ways to value cultural diversity in
the classroom. One way to do this begins with asking reflective questions.

- What do I know about the cultures that my students bring to school?
- Do I observe behaviors that differ from expectations in mainstream schools?
- How can I integrate cultural diversity as a building block in my classroom to improve learning for
  all students?

There are subtle ways that cultural diversity is evident in
the classroom. For example, many African American and Latino students, especially if they come from traditional cultural

backgrounds, engage in "getting ready" behaviors. They will need to sharpen a pencil, stretch their arms, and/or push the chair backward into a more comfortable position. These are called "preparation before performance" behaviors, and culturally responsive teachers understand these actions as part of the learning process and not an attempt to keep from working (Gay, 2000). Native American children may be particularly responsive to learning orally, as this is such a strong tradition in their culture (Pang, 2005). Children from an Oriental culture will not look a teacher in the face because that would be a sign of disrespect; we, on the other hand, tell children to "look at me." Latino children work particularly well in cooperative learning settings.

Teachers who look closely at the students in their classrooms affirm diversity with valuing actions. We participate in equity audits to look at data to see if all children are participating equally in clubs, extracurricular activities, and advanced classes. We observe on the playground and in the lunchroom to notice if all children are being included. We invite people from different backgrounds to speak in our classrooms and share their rich experiences. We integrate literature that emphasizes different cultures into the curriculum. We build on the rich experiences of children who speak more than one language. After all, in Texas, for example, language minority speakers are 14% of the student population.

We affirm a student's cultural heritage by listening to the music of the culture. For example, in San Antonio, a dance routine called stepping, based on a 100-year-old tradition of African American dance, is offered in several schools as an alternative to traditional sports. The performances include singing, changing, line dancing, and some gymnastics. Stepping is founded in African lore when tribes stepped in ceremonies, such as weddings, funerals, and other religious rites (Davis, 2004).

Teachers form study groups and read and discuss books, such as:

- ◆ Carter, F. (1976). *The education of Little Tree*. Albuquerque: University of New Mexico Press.

- Chen, D. (1999). *Colors of the mountain.* New York: Anchor Books.

- Delpit, L. (1995). *Other people's children.* New York: The New Press.

- Howard, G. (1999). *We can't teach what we don't know.* New York: Teachers College Press.

- Kohl, H. (1994). *I won't learn from you.* New York: The New Press.

- Kozol, J. (2000). *Ordinary resurrections* New York: Perennial.

- Lindsey, R.B., Roberts, L.M., & Campbell-Jones, F. (2005). *The culturally proficient school.* Thousand Oaks, CA: Corwin Press

- Nasdijj (2000). *The blood runs like a river through my dreams.* Boston: Houghton Mifflin.

- Tatum, B. (1997). *Why are all the black kids sitting together in the cafeteria?* New York: Basic Books.

Celebrating cultural diversity through special days or weeks is a place to begin. But to acknowledge, affirm, and really celebrate cultural diversity, we must understand our students through the diverse experiences they bring to school.

Be about Crossing Bridges

Culturally responsive teaching is not just an issue of race or ethnicity. Our cultural influences are far greater and extend to gender, socioeconomics, age, sexual identity, physically challenging conditions, and many more. Recently, I was appointed chairman of the spring lecture series at our university. The speaker the committee selected was the actress Marlee Matlin. I was responsible for Marlee for the afternoon and evening while she was on our campus.

I had never spoken with anyone who was deaf. How would we communicate? As I welcomed Marlee, I wondered, what should I do? Should I speak louder? Should I speak more slowly? How did I make eye contact? Should I reach out and touch her? What if she spoke, and I offended her if I couldn't understand? As she exited the car, I welcomed Marlee with a handshake and an idiotic grin. With her interpreter, Bill Pugin, we made our way to the library, where she would conduct a question–answer session with students. With every step, my mind focused on Marlee's *disability* and my *inability*.

As she interacted with students, I watched Marlee frequently voicing her responses, but always signing. Her hands moved through the air with an elegant eloquence. She was humorous, then serious, and always respectful as she responded thoughtfully to student questions. Then, the book signing began. Whether students handed her the book or a piece of paper, she looked directly at them with a welcoming smile and often wrote a brief message along with her name. She smiled and posed for pictures. She communicated beautifully with the students, both hearing and nonhearing. By now, I was becoming less tense. I quit thinking so much about *disability* and *inability* and instead began to observe dimensions of communication *ability* that I had not noticed before.

Following this session, we joined others for dinner. It had been a long day already, and all of us were hungry. Still, the conversation was lively around the table. While I was still a bit nervous, I was actually more curious. Next on the agenda was the evening lecture. Communicating in the small sessions had not been a problem. But how would Marlee keep the attention of a crowd of 500 when she would sign and Bill would be her voice?

Marlee and Bill walked on to the stage. Despite her small stature, her presence dominated the stage, and she began her speech. After the first few sentences, I no longer differentiated between Marlee's signing and Bill's voice. Instead, I heard her words. I laughed when she said something funny and was disappointed to hear of challenges she faced. She spoke eloquently and with passion about being raised as a child, not as a deaf child. About being an actress, not a deaf actress. About being a woman, not a deaf woman. About *ability*, not *disability* or *inability*.

At one point, Marlee told of a sign that her father placed in her neighborhood when she was young so that drivers would slow down. It read "Deaf Child Crossing." This phrase kept repeating in my mind and what a vivid mental picture it presented! I could see this child who was deaf, crossing not a street but a bridge leading from one world into another, a hearing and speaking world, full of diverse challenges—a world that would make her life much richer.

After Marlee's speech, she sat at a table to once again sign autographs. I stood beside her, placing the books and papers in front of her and telling her what to write on each one. We worked in comfortable rhythm. After a while, she reached in her purse and took out a piece of gum. She was not looking at me, so I gently touched her arm, and asked for a piece. For over an hour, she signed her name, hugged babies, smiled for photographs, listened respectfully as people thanked her for her work, told her she was beautiful, and gave dozens of other compliments.

I watched the crowd of admirers. Both hearing people and nonhearing people waited in line to share their joy at Marlee's presence. A mother who had driven two hours from Houston brought her 5-year-old son and daughter who were deaf to meet Marlee. A father who was deaf signed proudly as he introduced his children to her. I had not realized there were so many people in our community who were hearing impaired. How many times on campus had I passed students who were signing, yet I had not spoken? Had their silence made them invisible to me?

I thought again of the phrase Deaf Child Crossing. But this time I did not think of inability or disability, but of ability. I didn't think of Marlee, but of myself. I was the one crossing from my hearing, speaking side of the bridge to another world. This new world was filled with people whose silence was loud with laughter and with living. This was a new culture with new, diverse challenges and rich with learning—a world that would make my life much richer.

I teach in a time when the world's communities are no longer separate from one another. When one school district in Houston has more than 200 languages and dialects spoken, when Somali children in a San Antonio classroom communicate by clicking in an unwritten language, when a child dressed in a chador walks beside a child wearing a mini-skirt,

when a child who is autistic is mainstreamed, when neighborhood schools are resegregating, when Native American children still live in abject poverty, when living room televisions
capture the horror of a tsunami on foreign shores. I teach social justice—the importance of celebrating diversity, respecting differences, and emphasizing ability over disability. Celebrating diversity demands that we connect with others by
communicating and building valuing relationships. Because I
understand the importance of making these connections, I
have always considered myself to be a bridge builder.

But this event reminded me that it is not enough to *build*
bridges. Teachers must be about *crossing* bridges—connecting
our separate worlds, and extending our abilities to communicate in diverse and rich ways. As a child, Marlee's parents encouraged her to go beyond her world—to overcome challenges presented by deafness. They did not see her particular
challenge as "at risk" but instead as "at potential." She was
taught not to emphasize *disability* but to explore *ability.* The
Deaf Child Crossing sign represented the delightful discovery
of crossing from one valued world to another valued
world—and crossing, and crossing, and crossing yet again.

After the lecture series the next day, as I walked on campus, I passed a group of students who were deaf. They were
signing animatedly. This time I did not look away; their silence shouted at me, and I could no longer ignore what I could
not hear. Instead, I felt a huge smile come to my face, and I
spoke "Hello." I was crossing a bridge named Diversity—and
it connected many worlds—and enriched them all with new
discovery.

There is a frightening dynamic that can occur in the classroom when teachers do not openly live the moral creed of accepting and affirming *every* child. Students who are not being
affirmed or accepted begin to feel inferior, while students who
are being affirmed and accepted begin to feel superior, creating an unhealthy environment for every child in the room.
"Bigotry is being certain of something you know nothing
about" (Bullivant, 2004). The classroom is a wonderful place
to combat the ignorance in prejudice, bias, and bigotry, and
teachers do this when they build affirming relationships with

students and provide opportunities for students to build positive relationships with one another.

Tactical Actions That Demonstrate Culturally Responsive Teaching

What tactical actions that demonstrate culturally responsive teaching do teachers implement to build relationships that value others?

- Understand your own identity.
- Confront biases in yourself.
- Confront biases in the classroom.
- Encourage appreciation among students for differences.
- Notice the level of involvement of all students.
- Ensure that diversity is integrated throughout the curriculum.
- Invite guest speakers into the school who have diverse backgrounds.
- Be sensitive to language barriers.
- Be sensitive to different abilities.
- Emphasize ability, not disability or inability.
- Challenge faculty to continue learning about cultural influences on themselves, students, and other faculty members.
- Have a classroom that is welcoming to all students and their parents.
- Read about individuals who represent different cultures.
- Incorporate diverse art forms into the classroom curriculum.

Driving in East Texas, I could see ahead of me that the tall pine trees stood on either side of the road as guardians of my travel. As I drove, I noticed, because of the distance, that the green of the trees was made up of a myriad of shades. Some greens were deep and dark, others were light, and some lighter still. As I drove closer to the trees, I could see that most of these trees shared a similar shade of green. It was only when seen through the sunlight that their limbs shimmered with a diverse array of greens.

Nature was presenting me with a lesson, not about trees, color, and sunlight—but about diversity in relationships. Like the tree, on the surface people are much the same. We eat, work, laugh, cry, sleep, and so on. But it is not until we acknowledge cultural influences that we begin to appreciate the richness and depth of our diversity. As I looked at the trees—the same tree covered in shade was dark green, when the sun shone, the leaves were light, when rain sprinkles fell on the leaves—they shimmered as though dipped in silver. When the wind blew—the leaves moved and danced and looked altogether different.

The same tree, the same leaf, the same—but different. Was this a deficit? On the contrary, each tree became a living, glowing piece of welcoming art, sheltering my car as it drove down an unfamiliar highway. When teachers make the most of each moment to demonstrate culturally responsive behavior in the classroom, they understand themselves, they confront prejudice and bias in themselves and in the classroom, they acknowledge and affirm cultural diversity, and they lead the way in crossing bridges that lead to discovery. All of these actions lead to building relationships that value others. Hector and Maria, in the brief time I knew them, helped me begin to understand the richness of the mosaic of moral purpose that would shape my actions as a teacher.

Remember, BRAVO teachers build relationships with actions that value others by demonstrating culturally responsive teaching.

Actions that Demonstrate
Culturally Responsive Teaching
The Mosaic of Moral Purpose

- Confront Personal Biases
- Confront Biases in the Classroom
- Acknowledge and Affirm Cultural Diversity
- Be about Crossing Bridges

7

Actions That Are Courageous— Fragile Blossoms in the Snow

Courage is not the towering oak that sees storms come and go. It is the fragile blossom that opens in the snow.

Alice MacKenzie Swaim

It has been a long day. I stand at the door willing the clock to reach 3:00 so that we can go home. I watch the second graders. My eyes fall on Ashley, who sits at her desk reading. She holds the book so close to her face that her nose touches the page. Her hair is dark brown, and her eyes are huge, behind thick glasses. Still, she only sees vague suggestions of shadow—she is almost blind. Ashley cannot hear the noises of her classroom: chairs scraping the floor, the other 7-year-olds talking and laughing, for she is deaf, also. When she walks, her gait is slow and sometimes unsteady because of illness.

I walk into the room and kneel beside Ashley's desk. She knows that I am near, because I place my hand on her arm. She turns from her reader and places her hand on mine. With a smile of joy she looks at me and squeezes my hand. "I am reading," she says in her deep, raspy voice. "I love to read at school."

In the busy moments of the school day, cluttered with activity and the scheduled confusion of teaching and learning, I rest my eyes on this child. This little girl, whose fragile world is quiet and muted in shadow, finds a sanctuary of hope at school and embraces it with courage. In her presence, I am renewed, and I do not hear the bell ringing to signal the end of another school day.

When I ask teachers to describe the ideal teacher, they use a wide variety of words: creative, kind, caring, humorous, flexible, good communicator, loving, stern, fair, patient, responsible, encourager, planner, and many more. Rarely, if ever, do I hear them say that teachers should be courageous. Yet, the effect a teacher has on a child is monumental because it is teachers who make a difference in student learning.

A government study suggested that teachers are responsible for as much as 18% of the changes of student test scores (Rowan, Correnti, & Miller, 2002). Another study reported that students who have a highly effective teacher have two additional months of academic achievement (Sanders & Rivers, 1996), whereas other studies have found that students who have highly effective teachers several years in a row score much higher on tests than other students (Rivers, 2000). For example, Babu and Mendro (2003) found that although low-achieving fourth-grade students' who had effective teachers three years in a row were twice as likely to pass the seventh-grade math test, these students were twice as likely to be assigned to ineffective teachers.

Then, of course, we know that students who are not successful in school or live with other risk factors, such as high poverty, are more likely to drop out without graduating from high school. For example, nationwide graduation rates for Native American, Latino, and African American students are only around 50%. In Texas, one of every two children participates in the federal free or reduced-price lunch program, one in every seven children has limited English proficiency, and the majority of students are children of color (Scheurich & Skrla, 2003). In a few years, it is these children who will be working at meaningful employment—or not working. How will students get good jobs if they are not educated well? Educating all children for success is not just important to teachers, it is important to our nation. Courage is at the heart of good teaching.

Teaching is a hard job, and it is emotionally draining. As teachers, we often get so caught up in the act of teaching, and frustrated by its challenges, that we lose hope, which erodes our courage to continue. Even today, I regain courage to continue teaching when I reflect on the courage that 7-year-old Ashley, like that fragile blossom in the snow, demonstrated daily as she struggled to learn. Teachers who demonstrate courage build valuing relationships with students by advocating for all students and by abounding in hope.

Advocate with Courageous Actions for Others

Raul moved from Mexico and enrolled at a small rural school in the South when he was in the eighth grade. He was placed in classes with 24 other eighth graders; there was no ESL or bilingual help available to him; and it was obvious from his first day that he was very frustrated. His eighth-grade teacher spoke no Spanish. After the first week, she told a fellow teacher that she just did not have time to work with "someone who doesn't even understand the language. I was hired to teach eighth grade, not to teach Spanish." Because the district was small, all grades from K–12 were on the same campus. John Smith, who spoke Spanish very well, had been teaching ninth and tenth graders at the rural school for two years. Hearing about Raul, he went to the principal and suggested that Raul attend his class, and he would work with him on English after school. The principal turned down both suggestions.

After two weeks, Raul rarely came to school. John Smith visited his home and talked with the boy and his parents. They told him that Raul had been a very good student in Mexico, but now they could not make him come to school. John went back to the principal and requested again that Raul be allowed to attend his classes. Still, the principal turned him down. He waited a week and went back again with the same request. This time he brought Raul's parents who spoke no English to the meeting. Reluctantly, the principal gave his permission. It took courage, but John Smith knew that someone had to advocate for Raul.

America's children need an advocate. According to the Children's Defense Fund (2004):

♦ One in six children lives in poverty.

♦ One in eight children—9.3 million—have no health insurance.

♦ Only 32% of fourth graders read at or above grade level.

♦ An estimated 3 million children were reported as suspected victims of child abuse and neglect.

♦ Almost 1 in 10 teens ages 16 to 19 is a school dropout.

♦ Eight children or teens die from gunfire in the United States each day—one child every three hours.

Each day in America

♦ Five children or teens commit suicide.

♦ 366 children are arrested for drug abuse.

- 2,171 babies are born into poverty.
- 2,341 babies are born to mothers who are not high school graduates.
- 2,455 children are confirmed as abused or neglected.
- 2,539 high school students drop out.
- 4,440 children are arrested.
- 17,072 students are suspended (Children's Defense Fund, 2004).

America's children need advocates, but so do the children of the world. It takes courage, but if teachers do not advocate for our children, who will? Recently, I attended a conference where Minnie Jean Brown-Trickney spoke. Minnie Jean is one of the nine African American students who integrated the high school in Little Rock, Arkansas in 1957. She said, "There is weeping and moaning at the way things are in 2004 . . . Our children are the mirror of our society—listen to them." Then she challenged educators: "You have to speak—Do not remain silent" (University Council of Educational Administration, 2004). As an advocate, we build relationships with each student when we recognize their potential and emphasize resilience.

Recognize Potential

Recently, my brother-in-law Gary found his first-grade class picture. Although I was not in that picture, I went to high school with the same people. We began looking at the old black-and-white photo. Could I guess who that was? What about this one? And, oh look, here she is. And then it struck me—this old photograph that had captured a moment in time nearly 50 years ago was a picture of tremendous potential. Twenty 6-year-olds, girls in braids and dresses, boys in jeans and crew cuts, looked beyond the photographer and into the future. There was a boy who grew up to head one of America's largest insurance agencies, there was a girl who charied a science department at a well-known university, this one became an attorney, this one a judge, this one a medical doctor, this one a teacher, and this one a soldier who did not return from

Vietnam. The children in this picture grew up to become mothers and fathers, and now even grandparents; they helped others, voted, and showed courage in adversity.

Had our teachers been aware of this explosion of potential? If they heard today how successful these baby-faced 6-year-olds have become, what would be their reaction? Would they say, "I thought so, I always told him he could do it." Or would they say, "I had no idea she was that capable. I'm very surprised!" Did they view teaching, like Michelangelo, who took a block of marble and "released the statue from the stone." Or, as Anne Frank, "Everyone has inside of him a piece of good news. The good news is that you don't know how great you can be! How much you can love! What you can accomplish! And what your potential is!" (http://borntomotivate.com)

Where were the teachers for Ben Carson, the worst student in the fifth-grade class? You remember Ben—the other students called him "dummy." Dr. Ben Carson is now director of pediatric neurosurgery at the Johns Hopkins Medical Institutions in Baltimore, Maryland. But, after seeing his poor grades, his mother, who had only a third-grade education, required him to read two books a week and write book reports. She could not even read his reports. But, by sparking his interest in reading, he began to explore his interest in science. Dr. Carson said, "When I was in the fifth grade I thought I was stupid. So I conducted myself like a stupid person. And I achieved like a stupid person.... When I was in the seventh grade, I thought I was smart. So I conducted myself like a smart person, and achieved like a smart person" (Quindlen, 2004, p. 1).

We look at the children in our classrooms and see children of poverty, children who do not understand the language, children who are contemplating suicide, children who are in abusive homes, children who are hungry, children who are homeless, children who are angry, children who are ignored, children who are bullied, children who are immigrants, children who misbehave, and children who are not learning. Herbert Kohl (1994) reminds teachers that we "reproduce failure" in some children and a "false sense of superiority in others" when we limit our vision to a child's environment or economic status (p. 44). Despite their circumstances all of our children want to be successful. Inside their fragile souls are poets, musicians, artists, teachers, lawyers, mothers, fathers, builders, soldiers, salesmen, farmers, doctors, and scientists. All of them are waiting for a teacher with courage who will advocate for them and recognize their potential. Our students cry out for teachers who, as Goethe, said will "treat [them] as if they were what they ought to be and…help them to become what they are capable of being" (http://www.borntomotivate.com).

Emphasize Resilience

I consider myself an optimistic, positive person, but when I read the newspaper or watch the news, I am reminded that we live in tough times. When I wrote my doctoral dissertation 15 or so years ago, one of the questions that I asked teachers concerned the stresses that make teaching difficult. Nearly all of them said that what made teaching most difficult were those life circumstances such as poverty, violence, and poor quality of home life that teachers really couldn't do anything about. In the years since that time, I often ask teachers that if this is so, why do we continue teaching? Invariably, they answer with something about the resilience of their students. And they are right, studies have shown that even among children exposed to serious, high-risk factors, resilience often protects them from developing many of the problems that are predicted for them (Henderson & Milstein, 2003). Resilience is the ability to bounce back from difficult circumstances and resilient children and resilient adults have similar characteristics that include:

- ◆ Giving of oneself in serving others
- ◆ Possessing good life skills—decision making, assertive
- ◆ Having the ability to form positive relationships
- ◆ Having a good sense of humor
- ◆ Having Internal control

- Having a sense of independence
- Maintaining a positive view of the future
- Being flexibl
- Connection to learning
- Being self-motivated
- Feeling personal competence
- Possessing self-confidence (Henderson & Milstein).

This is a long list, and children and adults do not need every one of these characteristics to be resilient—that's how strong the inner drive is to move from risk to resilient. That is how much all children want to be successful.

Courageous teachers are a key to helping children become more resilient, when they model the characteristics of resiliency in their own lives, and also when they create an environment in the classroom that emphasizes the following steps:

- Increase bonding to school and academic accomplishment.
- Set clear and consistent boundaries.
- Teach life skills, such as cooperation, conflict resolution, assertiveness, communication, problem solving, and stress management.
- Provide caring and support through respect and encouragement.
- Set and communicate high expectations that are realistic.
- Provide opportunities for meaningful participation (Henderson & Milstein).

Consider Wilma Rudolph. She was born in poverty, the 20th of 22 children. At four, she had double pneumonia and scarlet fever, which left her with a paralyzed and useless left leg. She had to wear a leg brace, but her mother told her that she was very bright and could do whatever she wanted to do with her life. When Wilma was nine, she removed the brace and began to walk.

Four years later, she decided that she would like to be the world's greatest runner. She entered her first race at age 13 and came in last. She entered every high school race, and always came in last. But she kept trying, and one day she won a race and never lost again. She went to Tennessee State University and met a coach who saw her talent and trained her so well that she went to the Olympic Games. Her opponent that year was Jutta Heine, the world's greatest woman runner of the day. She beat Jutta in the 100-meter and 200-meter dashes. Finally, it was time for the 400-meter relay. When Wilma's teammate handed the baton to Wilma, she was so excited that she dropped it. Jutta was way ahead. Wilma picked up the baton, and ran into the history books as she won her third Olympic gold medal. Resilience.

I don't know much about football, but I love to watch it, especially college football. I am always amazed when teams fall far behind. If that were me, I'm sure I'd just say, "Coach, I think I'll take an early shower and head for home." But these guys just keep playing. The quarterback looks for somewhere to throw that ball, even when those huge players are running directly at him. Now, that takes courage. But they come right back out on the field for the next inning, quarter, half, or whatever football calls it. The players keep getting tackled, and they keep running, but they just keep bouncing back. But if you watch the coaches on the sidelines, you will see coaches advocating for students, recognizing potential, and emphasizing resilience. What are they doing? They clap, pat them as they run by, encourage "you can do it," and teach "next time, run this pattern," affirm "it's okay, try it again," tousle their hair, and give them a hug.

Teachers' classrooms are not stadiums, but we are very much like coaches on the sidelines. Just watch us. We smile, hug, and pat their shoulder, offer a word of encouragement, acknowledge how hard students are working, provide support when it is needed, affirm a student's efforts, connect a student to something interesting, write interesting comments on their papers, we urge our students every day in small ways that are not televised. It takes courage to nurture courage, but when we do, we build relationships that value students by advocating for them, recognizing their potential, and emphasizing resilience.

Abound in Hope

I serve on a committee for a scholarship called San Antonio Youth Educational Scholarship Foundation (SA YES) , sponsored by Dick and Lana Breakie. As part of the scholarship application, graduating high school seniors write a brief essay that describes why they should be considered. Applicants write about their need, and I am amazed at the resilience of these young people. Many are children of immigrants, and some are immigrants themselves. Many of these young people live with only one parent, and often they are the sole support for their families. In some ways, their stories are heartbreaking because they have suffered so much at such young ages. But they are so full of hope. They hope to become doctors, lawyers, architects, engineers, and teachers. They may not have much money, and they may already be too acquainted with struggle, but they believe in themselves, in the power of education, and in their ability to work hard for a better life. They are hopeful. One child of migrant parents wrote of her difficulty as a student—moving from school to school. She would just begin to get used to her surroundings when the family would move again. Then one year, she had a teacher who spoke no Spanish but greeted her every day with "Hola!" She wrote, "I decided that day I would learn how to read just like every other Anglo in my class."

Another student grew up with violence in her home. She wrote that "to be me, fragile is not even a word to describe, but strong is what I had to be." She went on to say that "ever since I was a young girl I realized the effect that a teacher would have in many children's lives. I began to want to have that same effect...." These young people and so many others, live what Emily Dickinson described so lyrically: "Hope is the thing with feathers that perches in the soul—and sings the tunes without the words—and never stops at all" (Matthiessen, 1950, p. 419).

Herbert Kohl (1994) describes an experience when he was a fifth grader. He was doing nothing in class. One day his teacher, in a casual conversation with him, asked what he was thinking about in social studies when he "hid behind [his] book." He told her that he was "pretending I'm in the pictures on the page." His teacher said that she thought it was wonderful that he was so imaginative, and perhaps one day he would draw or write about these things. Kohl says that, "That one moment when she revealed that she saw something in me worth honoring and respecting was the highlight of my elementary school career" (p. 82). The birth of hope.

I know a very successful, respected teacher, who was discouraged from going to college because most of her teachers did not think she was "capable." One day a teacher said, "I know one thing, you've certainly got the courage to make it through." That is all it took. Just one teacher's support, and she mailed an application the next day.

My colleague, Sandra Lowery, tells of moving frequently as a child, so that she had been in 11 high schools between her freshman year and senior year. When she tried to enroll as a senior in a new school, the high school counselor advised her to drop out of high school. Her grandmother said, "Of course you will not drop out, you will finish high school. I have high hopes for you." Well to make a long story short, 20 years later she replaced that high school counselor, then later went on to become a principal, superintendent, and university professor.

Writer and Holocaust survivor, Elie Wiesel reminds us "Just as despair can come to one only from other human beings, hope, too, can be given to one only by other human beings" (http://www.borntomotivate.com). Teachers instill hope in their students. We do this when we talk with our students and their parents to understand their hopes and dreams. Our actions also give hope to students when we offer grace to our students, and when we commit to stay the course. Teachers are dealers in hope.

Offer Grace

The students in my doctoral classes were asked to write about how they had changed over the course of their studies.

One of the students, Jim Vaszauskas, wrote about how he began to see education through the concept of grace—a gift, free of charge, and often undeserved; how "grace finds beauty in everything; grace finds goodness in everything." He then told of a time as a ninth grader when a teacher had complimented him, even though it was undeserved. He credits her offer of grace in recognizing his potential as a primary reason that he is an avid reader today.

Sometimes we just sort of stumble into grace. When my own daughter, Jamey, was in the third grade, she had a very young, very new, very good teacher with high standards and expectations for the children. At that time, Jamey was attending a Christian school, and every week the children memorized verses of scripture. She was a good student, but very shy. At home, we would practice her verse, and she would say it perfectly. But when it was time to say it for her teacher, she could not remember a word and kept making zeroes. Finally, I asked her teacher about this, and she told me that Jamey just obviously did not know the verse, not even the first word. I asked her to tell me how she tested the children. She explained that she would have the child come back to her desk where it was quiet and simply repeat the verse to her. If they couldn't say it, they got a zero. I asked if she gave them prompts, for example, did she tell them the first word to help them get started? She said, "Of course not. They either know the verse or they don't."

I thought for a minute and said, "Would you do me a favor this week, if Jamey cannot say any of her verse, would you just give her the first word. . . and see what happens?" I don't think she liked the idea, but she said that she would consider trying this.

Friday came, and on the way to school, Jamey said her verse perfectly to me. When she got to class, she was called back to the teacher's desk, and just as in previous weeks, her mind went blank. She couldn't say one word. But, this time her teacher told her the first word, and Jamey rattled off the entire verse. The teacher did this that day for other students, and sure enough, students that she thought did not know their verses at all soon were making 100s.

The following year, Jamey's teacher moved from Texas to Florida, and we lost touch. About 10 years later, one day my telephone rang, and it was this teacher. Her young daughter had just started first grade, and she wanted to share with me that now as a mother of a shy, little girl, she fully understood why it had been so important to offer grace to her students.

When teachers have the courage to offer grace to our students, we give them hope. When we build relationships with our students and get to know their strengths and weaknesses, we value who they are. Grace is a gift that expands the soul with hope for the giver and the receiver: the teacher and the student.

Stay the Course

Teachers are important people. We know that teacher turnover has a negative effect on student achievement. Yet, schools with 50% or more minority students experience turnover at twice the rate of schools with lower minority populations (NCES, 1998) and schools with poverty levels greater than 50% have significantly higher rates of turnover (Ingersoll, 2001). We also know that 20% of new teachers leave after only three years and 30% quit after five years (Ingersoll). Within seven years, 40% of all new teachers drop out of teaching, identifying student discipline problems and little support from colleagues as a major concern (Mills, Moore, & Keane, 2001).

Further research suggests that underqualified teachers are most likely to teach in high need areas, while in California up to 40% of emergency-permit teachers left the profession within a year (Darling-Hammond & Sykes, 2003). Then, of course, there are teachers who have been teaching for 10 and 15 years who just get tired and burn out.

Those of us who enter teaching because we want to help children must constantly remember that our students need us, and we must stay the course despite the difficulty of our job. The poet A. E. Housman tells of having whole stanzas of a poem flash into his mind one day while he was standing on a street corner waiting to cross. What came to him without any conscious effort on his part was a poem—an unfinished poem.

Yet it took him six months to write the last two stanzas of that poem" (Hughes, 1980, p. 4). Realizing that the most delicate, exquisite line of poetry may have been literally agonized into creation should help us as teachers to stay with the struggle through those difficult teaching times. Times when it just doesn't seem to come together the way we think it should.

Over the years, I cannot count the number of times I have heard students of all ages come up to teachers and ask, "Will you be here next year?" How can we encourage students to keep trying, to not give up, if our actions don't model the same staying power that we ask them to have? This is all the more reason why we need to develop strong supportive relationships with our students—who will encourage us, just as we encourage them. The collaborative relationships that we develop with parents and with other teachers are especially valuable because they provide a support to see us through the difficult times.

I remember a year that I had a particularly difficult class. I had come back to teaching in December after my daughter was born. Of course, I was torn leaving my 6-month-old baby with a babysitter, but it was necessary. My class assignment was teaching sixth-grade remedial math, which I had never taught before. The students really had run off two teachers before me. All right, pretend I didn't say that. Two teachers before me had left. There was no discipline in the class, and if there had been chandeliers they really would have been hanging from them! The students felt like the rejects of the school, which, unfortunately, they were. I felt rejected being given this class, and I worked very hard at establishing myself as teacher in control.

After one particularly bad day, I went home in tears; but because it had been so wild in the classroom all day, I don't think my students went home very happy either. The next day when the students came in, they started to get out their math books and I said, "Not today." They looked at me in surprise, and the room actually got quiet. Then I began to talk with them about how I was unhappy at coming back to school and leaving my new daughter. I told them that I wasn't enjoying our class because it was noisy and out of control, and I didn't feel that I was helping anyone. They just sat there, not saying a word. Then one of the girls said something about not wanting to be in this "bad, dumb class either." Others began talking—all of a sudden the students were expressing their disappointment and *talking*, not arguing, not shouting—just talking. And we even laughed *together*. That day was the beginning of something very special.

We began to bond as a group of people. We began to know one another. And we all discovered that we liked each other. By the end of the week, there was no more talk about this "bad, dumb class." We had forged a special relationship. It had taken courage to remove myself from the pedestal of a teacher in control to become their teacher, and it had taken courage for the students to open up to me, but we did. I made it through the year, and so did the students. We even learned quite a bit of math in the process. But most of all, we all learned about the power of building relationships that valued one another. When I came in December, the teacher down the hall had told me the class was "hopeless," but by February hope abounded in that classroom. I've never been sorry that I stayed.

Tactical Actions
That Demonstrate Courage

What tactical actions demonstrate courage that build relationships that value others?

- Speak openly about what you believe.
- Advocate for student learning.
- Advocate for student participation.
- Tell students and others what you see students do well.
- Actively look for potential talents in students.
- Bond with students by talking with them and getting to know them.
- Involve students in school activities that connect them to the school.

- Set clear, consistent boundaries and communicate these clearly.
- Use cooperative learning.
- Involve students in conflict resolution training.
- Teach students how to be appropriately assertive.
- Model and train students in communication skills.
- Provide opportunities for creative decision making.
- Openly care for your students.
- Establish high expectations for all students.
- Teach a hands-on curriculum.
- Involve students in goal setting.
- Extend grace to students.
- Listen to students.
- Give students a second chance.
- Do not give up.
- Model staying power.

BRAVO teachers are courageous when they stand up for children who need an advocate.

Sometimes teachers are the voice for struggling children, and sometimes they are the eyes. Unfortunately, all schools are not yet sanctuaries for all children, and for some, school is painful and difficult. Students progress at different rates and experience a myriad of stressors. For many of our children, school is a place where it takes courage just to come into the classroom. But when teachers make the most of each moment to become advocates for children, recognizing their potential and emphasizing resilience skills to help them bounce back from difficulty, schools become places that nurture courage. When schools abound in hope, they become places where teachers and students stay the course; where children like Ashley find a sanctuary, and their fragile souls flourish like the fragile blossom that pushes through the snow in winter.

Courage means they will not be denied their opportunity to bloom.

> "If you look for strengths and filter the world through the prism of hope, you will see and encourage the unexpected flowering of child life in the most unlikely places." (Kohl, 1994, p. 44)

Remember, BRAVO teachers build relationships with actions that value others by demonstrating courage.

Actions That Demonstrate Courage

Fragile Blossoms in the Snow

Advocate with Courageous Actions for Others
- Recognize Potential
- Emphasize Resilience

Abound in Hope
- Offer Grace
- Stay the Course

8

Relationships: The True Thread

"This is emergence—life exploring connections to create new and surprising capacity."

(Margaret Wheatley & Myron Kellner-Rogers, 1999, p. 53)

> *"You're almost as pretty as my mom."* I was delighted
> *with this compliment from Brenda, one of my fourth*
> *graders. I was 20, with long, straight blonde hair,*
> *stood 5 feet, 2 inches, weighed 100 pounds, and wore a*
> *mini-skirt that hit about 5 inches above my knee—I*
> *thought I looked pretty good, too!*

About a week later, Brenda walked into the classroom
with a huge smile on her face. "My mom's outside. I want you
to meet her." I brushed my hair, put on some fresh lipstick,
and walked outside to meet Brenda's mom.

Only one lady stood in the parking lot. But it couldn't be
Brenda's mom. This lady weighed at least 200 pounds and
had shoulders as broad as any professional linebacker's. She
wore a pair of too-short, too-tight shorts and a top so small
that most of her stomach was outside the top, hanging over
her shorts. Her hair was in curlers. She was barefooted and
wore no makeup. Even if she had, I'm afraid it wouldn't have
improved her appearance much.

I looked around the deserted parking lot, thinking, surely
there is some attractive young mother out here; but, no, it was
empty, except for Brenda, proudly holding the hand of her
mother who was "prettier" than I was.

This was in 1969, my very first week as a teacher. Although it took a while for me to fully understand what had
happened in that parking lot, today I still bask in the compli-
ment that Brenda gave me. She thought her teacher was almost as pretty as her mother. Brenda loved her mother and
saw her as beautiful, and she saw me through those same
eyes. When I realized the standard of love that Brenda used to
see beauty in me, I wanted even more to meet her expectations
and be a better teacher. I could see that our relationship as
teacher and student was beginning to grow, for it is our relationships with people that determine how we see one another
and ultimately how we live life.

Jesse Stuart was a teacher in the early 1900s. He worked
long hours at minimal pay and sometimes no pay at all. He
walked 17 miles in below-freezing weather to borrow books
for his students. He taught 54 separate lessons in one school
day to meet each child's need. He measured fields of corn to

demonstrate personal application to students. He painted the schoolhouse, washed the floor, started the fire, and poured lime in the outhouse. He collaborated with parents and the community to improve the school for his students. He built relationships with his students, and they became teachers and leaders in their communities. They left his classroom enthusiastic to do for others what he had done for them. He wrote:

> If every teacher in every school in America could inspire his pupils with all the power he had, if he could teach them as they had never been taught before to live, to work, to play, and to share, if he could put ambition into their brains and hearts, that would be a great way to make a generation of the greatest citizenry America had ever had.
> (Stuart, 1946, p. 87)

The book was titled *The Thread That Runs So True.* Today, that thread that runs so true builds relationships. As Margaret Wheatley (1999) said, "We live in a world where relationships are primary. Nothing happens in the quantum world without something encountering something else. Nothing exists independent of its relationships" (p. 69). Relationships thread their way through all that we do. As teachers, when our actions uphold high standards for all children, empower students, demonstrate our respect for them, support their learning, challenge their imaginations, acknowledge and affirm cultural diversity, and demonstrate courage, we create a tapestry of rich, colorful portraits of children. Years after we have taught them, we no longer remember all of their names, and we don't remember the skills that we taught, but we remember vividly the children and those moments we shared when together we created something that was very fine. Relationships are the thread that connects students to teachers.

One of my principal students told about a little boy in her class named Ryan, who had cerebral palsy and was unable to function without help. The teacher aide assigned to help Ryan was not in the room. As the teacher was reading a story to the class, she looked up from the book to see that Ryan had begun to noticeably drool. Without a second thought, a little girl got up from her chair, took a Kleenex from the box, and wiped his face. The child saw what Ryan needed, and gently and kindly met his need. Relationships are the thread that connects students to each other.

On December 26, 2004, a terrible tsunami hit parts of Asia. Almost immediately, nearly 200,000 people were declared dead, and millions more were missing. It was a horrific tragedy. But the newspaper was full of articles of children who were suffering and in need. School children throughout the world collected food and clothing for these survivors. Valuing others builds relationships across the miles; this is the thread that connects students to the world community.

My husband and I were flying to Ireland. The airplane cabin was quiet and dark as people were trying to sleep in the cramped quarters. I looked at my watch; it said 3:30 am. I could not sleep. We were only an hour away from London, so I knew that what appeared to be the dark of predawn night was really 9:30 on a sunny English morning. All I had to do was open the shade, and we would be flooded in sunlight. Sometimes as teachers, we often teach this way, willing our hard efforts to work, when only one small act would show us light. We create artificial circumstances, bring children into the schoolhouse, sit them in straight rows, put pencils in their hands and paper on their desks, tell them to listen, and expect to teach. But teachers build relationships when we learn about our students. We make the most of each moment by threading questions into the school day that explore who these childlike vessels of potential are, what they want to be, where they want to go, and how we can help them on their journey. When Brenda saw me through the eyes of someone she loved, I became more lovable. The thread that runs so true not only builds relationships that help the world look better but also that make a better world.

An 18-year-old immigrant girl from Mexico wrote in an essay that the day she came to America as an 8-year-old she made up her mind that "everything I do, no matter what shadow it may be under, will be an effort to live." She added, "It was my first teacher in my new land who showed me the way."

Robert Cooper (2001) tells the story of a Tibetan man who greeted him with the phrase *Tashi deley,* which means "I honor the greatness in you. I honor the place in you where lives your courage, honor, love, hope, and dreams." We only had a moment in Ireland to share our euros with a child missing a front tooth, but who knows where the actions of that moment may lead? When teachers make the most of each moment, no matter how small, to build relationships with actions that value others, we transform shadow into light, potential into life, and honor the greatness in our students—one student at a time, one family at a time, and one community at a time. Bravo, teachers!

Building Relationships with Actions That Value Others

Actions That Uphold High Standards for All
- Search Your Soul
- Accept Responsibility
- Create a Culture of Achievement

Empowering Actions
- Build Leadership Capacity
- Encourage Authentic Learning
- Demonstrate Democratic Principles

Respect for All Actions
- Be Fair
- Be Caring

Support Actions
- Communicate Effectively
- Encourage

Actions That Challenge the Imagination
- Be Open to Change
- Solve Problems Creatively

**Actions That Demonstrate
Culturally Responsive Teaching**
- Confront Your Own Personal Biases
- Confront Biases in the Classroom
- Acknowledge and Affirm Cultural Diversity
- Be about Crossing Bridges

Actions That Demonstrate Courage
- Advocate for Others
- Abound in Hope

9
References

Aronson, J. (2004). The threat of stereotype. *Educational Leader-ship, 62(3), 14–20.*

Babu, S., & Mendro, R. (2003, April). *Teacher accountability: HLM-Based teacher effectiveness indices in the investigation of teacher effects in a state assessment program.* American Education Research Association Annual Meeting: Chicago, IL.

Barth, R. S. (2003). *Lessons learned: Shaping relationships and the culture of the workplace.* Thousand Oaks, CA: Corwin Press.

benShea, N. (2003). *Inspire, enlighten, and motivate: Great thoughts to enrich your next speech and you.* Thousand Oaks, CA: Corwin Press.

Blankstein, A. M. (2004). *Failure is not an option: Six principles that guide student achievement in high-performing schools.* Thousand Oaks, CA: Corwin Press.

Blaydes, J. (2003). *The educator's book of quotes.* Thousand Oaks, CA: Corwin Press.

Booth, C. (1997). The fiber project: One teacher's adventure toward emergent curriculum. *Young Children, 52(4),* 79–85.

Bryk, A. S., & Driscoll, M. E. (1998). *The school as community: Theoretical foundation, contextual influences, and conse-quences for teachers and students.* Madison, WI: National Center for Effective Secondary Schools.

Bryk, A., & Schneider, B. (2002). *Trust in schools: A core resource for improvement.* New York: Russell Sage Foundation.

Bullivant, A. (2004). *The little book of humorous quotations.* New York: Barnes & Noble.

Canfield, J. & Hansen, M.V. (1996). *A 3rd serving of chicken soup for the soul.* Retrieved on April 24, 2005, from http://www.soupserver.com

Carr, C. (2004). A warrior for children. In S. Harris, J. Ballenger, F. Hicks-Townes, C. Carr, & B. Alford (Eds.), *Winning women: Stories of award-winning educators* (pp. 11–22). Lanham, MD: Scarecrow Education Press.

Children's Defense Fund. (2004). *State of America's Children 2004 Yearbook.* Washington, DC: Author.

Childress, S., & Johnson, D. (2004, Nov. 29). The hot sound of hate. *Newsweek, CXLIV (22), 32.*

Collins, J. (2004). *Good to great.* New York: HarperCollins.

Cooper, R. (2001). *The other 90%. New York: Three River Press.*

Cousins, N. Retrieved on December 19, 2004, from http://www.forbetterlife.org/value/quotes.asp?)

Darling-Hammond, L & Sykes, G. Wanted: A national teacher supply policy for education. *Education Policy Analysis Archives,* 11(33), 1–57. Retrieved September 22, 2003 from http://epaa.asu.edu/epaa/vlln33/

Davis, V. T. (2004, December 31). Stepping up to tradition. *San Antonio Express-News,* 1B.

Dewey, J. (1916). *Democracy in education: An introduction to the philosophy of Education.* New York: Macmillan.

Dewey, J. (1937). Democracy and educational administration. *School and Society,*45(1161), 457–462.

Eisen, A. (1995). *A woman's journey: Reflections on life, love, and happiness.* Kansas City, MO: Ariel Books.

Estes, C. P. (1992). *Women who run with the wolves.* New York: Ballantine Books.

Ewing Marion Kauffman Foundation. (2002). *Set for success: Building a strong foundation for school readiness based on the social-emotional development of young children.* Kansas City, MO: Author.

Fears, D. (2001, July 18). Schools' racial isolation growing. *The Washington Post,* A3.

Frank, A. Quotations. Retrieved December 20, 2004, from http://www.borntomitivate.com

Freire, P. (1998). *Pedagogy of Freedom: Ethics, Democracy, and Civic Courage.* Lanham, MD: Rowman & Littlefield.

Gay, G. (2000). *Culturally responsive teaching: Theory, research and practice.* New York: Teachers College Press.

Glasser, W. (1998). *Choice theory.* New York: HarperCollins.

Goethe, J. Quotations. Retrieved December 19, 2004, from http://www.borntomotivate.com

Gorrow, T. R. (2004). Rearrange your attitude: The art of being happy. *Back to School, 8*(1), 1–3.

Harris, S. (2000). Behave yourself. Good principals believe that leadership is at all levels of the school. *Principal Leadership, 1*(3), 36–39.

Harris, S. (2004). *BRAVO Principal: Building relationships with actions that value others.* Larchmont, NY: Eye On Education.

Harris, S. (2005) *Changing paradigms of educational leaders: Voices of students.* Lanham, MD: Scarecrow Education.

Harris, S., & Lowery, S. (2003). *Standards-based leadership: Case studies for the principal.* Lanham, MD: Scarecrow Education.

Harris, S., & Petrie, G. (2002). A study of bullying in the middle school. *NASSP Bulletin, 86* (633), 42–53.

Harris, S., Petrie, G., & Willoughby, W. (2002). Bullying among 9th graders. *NASSP Bulletin, 86*(630), 3–14.

Henderson, N., & Milstein, M. M. (2003). *Resiliency in schools.* Thousand Oaks, CA: Corwin Press.

Hodgkinson, B. (2003). Changing demographics—A call for leadership. In W. A. Owings & L. S. Kaplan (Eds.), *Best practices, best thinking, and emerging issues in school leadership,* (pp. 3–14). Thousand Oaks, CA: Corwin Press.

Hughes, R. (1980). How to write creatively. New York: Franklin Watts.

Ingersoll, R. M. (2001). Teacher turnover and teacher shortages: An organizational analysis. *American Educational Research Journal, 38*(3), 499–534.

Keller, H. Retrieved December 19, 2004, from http://ww.quotationspage.com

Kids Count 2004. (2004). *Data Book Online.* Retrieved on April 24, 2005, from http://www.aecf.org/kidscount/data book/indicators.htm

Kohl, H. (1994). *I won't learn from you.* New York: The New Press.

Lambert, L. (2003). *Leadership capacity: For lasting school improvement.* Alexandria, VA: Association of Supervision and Curriculum Development.

Matthews. L. J., & Crow, G. M. (2003). *Being and becoming a principal.* Boston: Allyn & Bacon.

Matthiessen, F. (1950), The Oxford Book of American Verse. NY: Oxford University Press.

Maturana, H. R., & Varela, F. J. (1992). *The tree of knowledge: The biological roots of human understanding.* Boston: Shambala.

McEntee (2004, Nov. 4). A community of kindness. *USA Today,* 6D.

Mills, H., Moore, D., & Keane, W. G. (2001). Addressing the teacher shortage: A study of successful mentoring programs in Oakland county, Michigan. *The Clearing House,* 74(3), 124–126.

National Center for Education Statistics (1998). *The condition of education.* (pp. 98–013). Washington, DC: U.S. Government Printing Office.

National Center for Education Statistics (2004). Retrieved on December 20, 2004, from http://nces.ed.gov/programs/digest/d03/tables/dt131.asp

National Parent Teacher Association. (1997). Retrieved on December 20, 2004, from www.pta.org/parentinvolvement/standards/index.asp

No Child Left Behind Act of 2001. Retrieved on December 20, 2004, from http:// www.nochildleftbehind.gov

Noddings, N. (1992). *The challenge to care in schools.* New York: Teachers College Press.

Pang, V. O. (2005). *Multicultural education: A caring-centered, reflective approach* (2nd ed.). Boston: McGraw-Hill.

Popham, W. J. (2005). Swords with blunt edges. *Educational Leadership,* 62(4), 86–87.

Quindlen, T. H. (Ed.). (2004). A journey from the bottom of the class to brain surgeon. *Education Update, 46* (4), 1. Alexandria, VA: Association for Supervision and Curriculum Development.

Quinn, D. (1992). *Ishmael.* New York: Bantam/Turner Books.

Rivers, J. C. (2000). *The impact of teacher effect on student math competency achievement.* (dissertation, University of TN, Knoxville) Ann Arbor, MI: University Microfilms International 9959317.

Rowan, B., Correnti, R., Miller, R. J. (2002). What large-scale research tells us about teacher effects on student achievement: Insights from the prospects study of elementary schools. *Teachers College Record, 104*(8), 1525–1567.

Sanders, W., & Rivers, J. C. (1996). *Cumulative and residual effects of teachers on students' future achievement.* Knoxville, TN: University of Tennessee Value-Added Research Center.

Scheurich, J. J., & Skrla, L. (2003). *Leadership for equity and excellence.* Thousand Oaks, CA: Corwin Press.

Sergiovanni, T. (1992). *Moral leadership* San Francisco: Jossey Bass.

Starratt, R. J. (2003) *Responsibility, authenticity and presence: Educational virtues for educational leaders.* Speech presented to Phi Delta Kappa meeting at Stephen F. Austin State University, November 15, 2003, Nacagdoches, TX.

Steinbeck, J. (1955). Like captured fireflies. *California Teachers Association Journal, 51*(7).

Stuart, J. (1940). *The thread that runs so true.* New York: Charles Scribner & Sons.

The Mouse Trap. Retrieved December 19, 2004, from http://www.indianchild.com/mouse.trap.htm

Trickney, M. J. (2004, November). Keynote speech. Annual conference of University Council of Educational Administration. Kansas City, MO: November, 2004.

Weiss, I., & Pasley, J. D. (2004). What is high-quality instruction? *Educational Leadership, 61*(5), 24–28.

Wheatley, M. (1999). *Leadership and the New Science.* San Francisco: Berrett-Koehler.

Wheatley, M., & Kellner-Rogers, M. (1999). *A simpler way.* San Francisco: Berrett-Koehler.

Wiesel, E. Quotations. Retrieved December 20, 2004, from http://www.borntomotivate.com

York-Barr, J. & Duke, K. (2004). What do we know about teacher leadership? Findings from two decades of scholarship. *Educational Research, 74* (3), 255–316.

For Product Safety Concerns and Information please contact our EU
representative GPSR@taylorandfrancis.com Taylor & Francis Verlag GmbH,
Kaufingerstraße 24, 80331 München, Germany

Printed and bound by CPI Group (UK) Ltd, Croydon, CR0 4YY

08/06/2025

01897003-0010